The Printer's Catch

An Artist's Guide to Pacific Coast Edible Marine Life

by

Christopher M. Dewees

Sea Challengers   1984   Monterey, CA

A Sea Challengers Publication

Front Cover: Redbanded rockfish, *Sebastes babcocki*

Photographs of original art by HARA

ISBN: 0-930118-10-3

Library of Congress Catalog Card Number: 83-051816

**Sea Challengers
4 Sommerset Rise
Monterey, California 93940**

Printed by Dai Nippon Printing Co., Ltd., Tokyo, Japan.

Phototypesetting and pre-press production by Padre Productions, San Luis Obispo, California.

Dedication

This book is dedicated to my wife, Christine, and to the memory of my mother, Sally. Christy's love, support, and patience made this book possible. My mother provided a loving childhood environment that encouraged my creativity, self-reliance, and confidence.

Table of Contents

Prints

Introduction

Fish have always been an important part of my life. As a child most of my spare moments were spent observing and catching fish in San Francisco Bay. My parents' love of sailboat racing always kept me near the water. My interest in fish and fishing grew: I became involved in commercial fishing, attended graduate school in fishery biology, and learned the art of Japanese fish printing.

This book combines art and nature. I have found that people who enjoy fish prints ("gyotaku") want to know more about the fish. Fishery scientists enjoy "gyotaku" as a unique scientific illustration method which gives a different perspective than drawings or photographs. Historically, successful fish printers have had a naturalist's background rather than an artist's. An understanding of fish structure, biology, and ecology is a vital prerequisite.

I have tried to cover most of the important Pacific Coast fish and shellfish families found between the California-Mexico border and Alaska. The book is not intended to be comprehensive. I've included at least one illustration for each family discussed. I combined a review of the scientific literature with my experience in marine fisheries to write the text. I am indebted to the many fine researchers and writers who have documented the biology of Pacific Coast fish and shellfish. Readers wanting more in-depth information can refer to the publications listed at the end of the book. I have minimized the use of technical terms and included a glossary and illustrations of common commerical fishing gear to help readers.

The illustrations for this book are all original fish prints done on handmade oriental papers. Because the prints are taken directly from the fish, an exact image of the organism is produced. I often prefer to work in black and white like a scientific illustrator, but in recent years I have begun to use more color to given an impression of the natural coloration of the fish. A detailed description of fish printing techniques is provided for those who want to try "gyotaku" for themselves.

I am indebted to many people for their help with this book. Tom Sharp introduced me to "gyotaku" in 1968, and we developed our techniques together through trial and error. Dan Gotshall provided encouragement and was willing to take the risk of publishing this unusual book. Eric Hochberg and Robert Little, who co-founded the U.S. Nature Printing Society, have been instrumental in the rapid growth of appreciation for fish and plant printing. Ken Hashagen did an excellent and thorough review of the manuscript.

A special thanks goes to my wife, Christine Marshall Dewees, who spent endless hours preparing my fish prints for display and reproduction, catching my numerous errors, and supplying constructive criticism. Her patience with fish-filled vacations and a fish-filled freezer was remarkable. Others who have made my work look good are Nicole Gibson and Christie Wyman, who sacrificed evenings and weekends to transform my terrible handwriting into a typed manuscript.

Finally, I want to thank the numerous people who have supplied fish and shellfish for me to print. Particularly helpful were the staff at California Academy of Sciences, Morgan and Benjamin Dewees, Bob Given and his staff at the U.S.C. Catalina Marine Science Center, Ken Gobalet, Ed Melvin, Peter Moyle, and Jim Waldvogel. Fish prints were loaned for reproduction in this book from the private collections of Jack Clark (shad, rosy rockfish), Jeanne Enos (striped bass) and Monica Seegars (wolf-eel).

Christopher M. Dewees
June 1984

SHARKS AND SKATES
Class Chondrichthyes

Life History

The sharks, skates, rays, and ratfish all have cartilaginous rather than bony skeletons. They are important predators of invertebrates and vertebrates and are currently becoming more heavily exploited by American fishermen.

Sharks and skates are found in all major habitat types along the Pacific Coast. They all carry out fertilization internally using the elongated claspers of the male. In general, they produce relatively few, but large, offspring. Some sharks and skates lay large eggs in leathery cases. Others hold the young in the uterus until they are fully developed, with nutrition supplied by an umbilical cord or from a yolk sac.

Sharks and skates are quite different from bony fish. The scales of these cartilaginous fishes develop like teeth and are very different from the scales of bony fish. Sharks don't have swimbladders, but this lack of buoyancy is overcome by the lightweight, cartilaginous skeletons and the bottom dwelling habits of many species (e.g. skates, rays, angel sharks). Unlike bony fishes who draw water across their gills by opening their mouths, sharks and skates usually have large openings (spiracles) that draw water into the gills.

The body forms of the sharks and rays are good indicators of their "lifestyle." The large, pelagic sharks such as the great white, mako, and blue have relatively streamlined bodies and forked tails, designed for fast swimming. These sharks prey primarily on fish, squid, and marine mammals. However, the two largest sharks in this group, the whale and basking sharks, strain plankton out of the water column.

At the opposite extreme, angel sharks, skates, and rays have flattened bodies that enable them to lie on the bottom with little energy expenditure while they wait to ambush their prey. Their large, wing-like pectoral fins enable them to swim surprisingly quickly. Some species, especially the bat ray, *Myliobatis californica*, flap their wings to uncover shellfish on soft bottoms. The shellfish are then crushed with the ray's flat, plate-like teeth.

The sharks and skates as a group tend to be slow-growing, long-lived, and have few offspring. This characteristic makes them vulnerable to overfishing. More complete life history information and careful fishery management are needed.

Fishery Information

Sharks and skates have long been ignored as a food source because of humans' negative attitudes about them. Most of the members of the Class Chondrichthyes are good to eat.

Sharks became the object of an intense fishery during World War II when high prices were paid for the livers, which are high in Vitamin A. War activities cut off traditional sources of Vitamin A such as cod liver oil from the North Atlantic. Shark populations, particuarly the soupfin shark, *Galeorhinus zyopterus*, were significantly reduced. By the mid-1940s synthetic Vitamin A was available cheaply. The fishery disappeared until the mid-1970s, when consumers developed a taste for the relatively inexpensive shark. Commercial fishermen, especially those in the erratic anchovy, swordfish, and salmon fisheries, turned to shark as a supplemental fishery.

Most of the landings come from southern California. The primary species landed are the thresher shark (*Alopias vulpinus*), shortfin mako (*Isurus oxyrinchus*), leopard shark (*Triakis semifasciata*), Pacific angel shark (*Squatina californica*), and blue shark (*Prionace glauca*). All except the blue shark are captured primarily in gillnets or trammel nets. Blue sharks are captured with longlines.

Along the rest of the Pacific Coast most of the landings are made in bays and nearshore waters with longlines or as part of the incidental catch of trawlers. The soupfin shark, spiny dogfish (*Squalus acanthias*), and the skates (*Raja* spp.) are commercially the most important sharks in northern waters. Sharks are also the object of a growing recreational fishery as anglers become more aware of their fighting ability and excellent eating quality.

Consumer Information

The meat of sharks and skates varies in texture from the dense, swordfish-like quality of the thresher shark to the soft texture of the blue shark. All sharks and skates *should be bled, gutted, and chilled immediately* after they are captured to insure top quality. Sharks concentrate urea in their body (especially in the blood) in high levels. If this urea is not removed quickly, the fish will have a strong ammonia-like odor and bitter taste.

Fresh shark is commonly seen in California markets because most of the Pacific Coast landings come from southern California. Fresh shark is most abundant during the summer and fall months. Steaks of the large thresher and shortfin mako (bonito sharks) and fillets of small species such as soupfin and leopard sharks serve as inexpensive alternatives to swordfish.

Due to its increased popularity, some shark is generally available in most Pacific Coast seafood markets. Some of the lesser known, but delicious, types include angel shark, dogfish, and sevengill. I prefer to barbecue or broil shark, often with a marinade. Skate "wings" are excellent when poached.

STURGEON
Family Acipenseridae

Life History

Two species of sturgeon occur in nearshore waters, estuaries, and coastal rivers along the Pacific Coast from northern California through Alaska. The green sturgeon, *Acipenser medirostris*, grows to 7 ft and 350 lb. The white sturgeon, *Acipenser transmontanus*, is the largest freshwater fish in North America, growing to 20 ft and well over 1,000 lb.

Sturgeon spawn in fresh water and spend much of their life in bays and the ocean. They grow slowly and females don't sexually mature until they are about 14 years old. Sturgeon live more than 50 years and some people claim that sturgeon live well over 100 years. Spawning takes place in the spring months in fresh water when 600,000 to 4,000,000 eggs are released. The young travel downstream and feed on invertebrates, herring eggs, and small fish throughout their lives.

Fishery Information

Because of their slow growth and late age of first maturity, sturgeon have historically been susceptible to overfishing. In the late 1800s, large commercial catches and habitat degradation decimated sturgeon populations. In California, the fishery was completely closed between 1917 and 1954. Since 1954 there has been a sport fishery in California for fish over 40 inches in length, a size which allows the fish to spawn at least once. With the introduction of live shrimp for bait, the sport fishery for sturgeon has become successful, especially in the San Francisco Bay area.

Today, the commercial fishery is centered primarily on the Columbia River, where approximately 10,000 sturgeon are landed each year. Both gillnets and longlines are used. The catch is limited to fish between 4 and 6 ft in length. This restriction protects first-time spawners and the older spawners who produce huge numbers of eggs. Researchers at the University of California at Davis are perfecting sturgeon culture techniques in order to produce 1½- to 2-lb sturgeon for smoking or sale as fresh fish and to commercially raise sturgeon to enhance wild sturgeon populations.

Consumer Information

Sturgeon has a very hard, dense flesh which has an excellent flavor. It can be smoked, barbecued, poached, or baked. Because it is a cartilaginous fish, bones are not a problem.

Most of the sturgeon resource is allocated to recreational fishermen, so sturgeon is seldom available in markets. A small commercial fishery takes place during the spring and summer on the Columbia River. Ask your seafood market manager when he can obtain sturgeon.

If you are lucky enough to catch a mature female, the fresh roe can be made into caviar rather simply. Use eggs less than 24-hr old. Remove the individual eggs from their sac and place them in a bowl. Make sure you remove all other materials. For each 1 or 2 cups of eggs, prepare a brine of 1/2 cup salt to 2 cups cold water. Pour eggs into brine and swirl. Let stand for 30 minutes. Pour caviar into a strainer and rinse with cold water. Remove any remaining membrane. Store caviar in a tightly closed container in the refrigerator. It should keep for several weeks.

HERRING
Family Clupeidae

Life History

This family includes the herring, sardine, and shad, which are important to both commercial and recreational fisheries. They all have compressed bodies with large, delicate silvery scales. Members of this family feed almost entirely on plankton found in surface waters along the Pacific Coast. Most are important forage fish.

The Pacific herring, *Clupea harengus pallasi*, ranges from northern Baja California to Alaska and Japan. Herring spawn in estuaries, where they attach their egg clusters to rocks, algae, and other solid objects. Spawning begins in November in California and is progressively later as one moves northward (June in Alaska). The herring form dense schools during the spawning season and tend to spawn during periods of high tides and high freshwater runoff. The eggs hatch in 6 to 11 days. The young fish migrate to the sea and, as adults, show a tendency to return to their birth place for spawning.

The second key member of this family, the American shad, *Alosa sapidissima*, is not native to the Pacific Coast. They were introduced from the Atlantic Coast into the Sacramento River during the 1870s and the Columbia River during the 1880s. By 1879 shad were common enough to appear in the commercial gillnet catch. Today they range from Baja California to Alaska. The American shad is the largest member of the herring family, growing to 30 inches. They are anadromous and spawn during the late spring and early summer in large Pacific rivers. Males mature younger (4 years) than females (5 to 6 years). Unlike salmon, shad return to the ocean and have been known to spawn seven consecutive years. The young spend their first summer in the river systems and then migrate to sea. Little is known about their ocean habits.

Fishery Information

Fisheries for members of the clupeid family have been important, wildly fluctuating, and at times controversial. Most clupeids lay large numbers of eggs and the survival rate of each year class fluctuates greatly and unpredictably. Oceanic conditions, availability of suitable food for the larvae, and interaction with other species all contribute to success of a year class. This wide fluctuation in abundance and their schooling behavior make the herring vulnerable to overfishing.

Historically, British Columbia has been the leading producer of herring, with landings often exceeding 200,000 tons. Along the rest of the coast herring has been a relatively minor fishery until the Japanese market for imported herring expanded during the early 1970s. Herring are now caught with purse seines and gillnets in bays along the entire coast. The roe is extracted and exported to Japan where it is known as "kazunoko." The fishery has become so valuable that complex limited entry programs and strict quotas have been im-

plemented to try to reduce the fishing effort and protect stocks. During the winter months, San Francisco Bay is often full of herring boats searching for mature spawning herring. Prices vary widely (up to $2,000 per ton of herring) and the prices are often based on the amount of roe per ton of herring.

A valuable fishery also exists for herring eggs attached to edible seaweed such as *Gracilaria* and *Laminaria*. Much of this is exported to Japan where it is a delicacy called "kazunoko kombu." A small amount of herring is also caught to be sold fresh or pickled. Sportsfishermen can also catch herring when they are spawning in shallow waters. They use dipnets, cast nets, or leaders with many small, feathered hooks. Large concentrations of seals, sea lions, and gulls are good indicators of the herring's presence during the spawning season.

The American shad fishery is primarily a recreational one, even though it is important commercially on the East Coast. Most shad are captured using brightly colored, weighted flies and small lures during the spring months when the shad ascend rivers for spawning. In California, a unique "bumping" method is also used at night in the Sacramento-San Joaquin River system. A long-handled, chicken-wire dip net is fished in the prop wash of a slow-moving boat. When a shad "bumps" the net, it is flipped up into the boat.

Consumer Information

Members of this family tend to be bony and high in fat content. The roe of both the herring and shad is excellent eating. Herring for human consumption are usually pickled or smoked. Increasing the human use of the carcasses from the herring roe fishery should be given attention. Shad is tasty fresh, but its numerous small bones make it difficult to fillet. Most anglers either release the shad alive or smoke those they keep.

Several types of pickled herring are available all year to consumers in markets. Fresh herring can be purchased during the winter and spring months when the commercial fishery takes place. The herring at this time tend to be lower in fat content because they have used up much of their resources in spawning.

Several members of this fish family, especially the Pacific herring and the threadfin shad, *Dorosoma petenense*, are valuable as bait for salmon and striped bass.

ANCHOVIES
Family Engraulidae

Life History

The northern anchovy, *Engraulis mordax*, is the most important member of this family along the Pacific Coast. The northern anchovy occurs from the tip of Baja California to Vancouver Island. There are apparently three subpopulations: Vancouver Island to San Francisco, San Francisco to central Baja California, central to southern Baja California. The central subpopulation is the most heavily exploited and studied.

Anchovies are small, silvery, pelagic fishes. They seldom grow to more than 7 inches in length. The adults mature between 12 and 24 months of age and they spawn many times during the year. Large females may spawn at least a dozen times each year. This reproductive strategy is the anchovy's way of avoiding complete failure of its fragile eggs and larvae in an unpredictable ocean environment.

Spawning peaks in late winter and the eggs hatch within 4 days. The delicate eggs and young are quite vulnerable to predation, starvation, and adverse oceanographic conditions. The success of each year class is quite variable and unpredictable.

Anchovies grow within 1 year to 4 inches in length. Young anchovies tend to be more common nearshore where they feed primarily on plankton. Anchovies are short-lived, with few surviving more than 4 years. Seven years of age and 7.9 inches in length are the maximums reported. The northern anchovy is important as forage for many large marine fishes, mammals, and birds. Anchovies are a particularly important food source for brown pelicans.

Fishery Information

Anchovies have been harvested commercially in California since 1916. Landings were relatively small until the failure of the sardine fishery during the early 1950s. By 1966 a substantial reduction fishery (processed into animal feed) was established. Landings since then have fluctuated widely between 11,000 and 156,000 tons annually.

The anchovy fishery is centered off Los Angeles with a smaller fishery in Monterey Bay. The vessels land fish primarily at San Pedro and Port Hueneme, where reduction processing facilities exist. The primary gear used is the purse seine. The same vessels may also fish for squid, mackerel, bonito, and other pelagic fishes.

There is also an important anchovy fishery supplying live bait for recreational fishermen. Vessels using lampara nets in nearshore waters land 7,000 to 8,000 tons annually in southern California and San Francisco Bay. This fishery is worth more than $2 million annually.

Management of this fishery is complex because of the difficulty of estimating the population size, controversy over allocation of the resource, and the volatile market for anchovy products. Anchovy management is influenced by memories of the collapse of the sardine fishery in 1952. Like sardines, anchovies are a pelagic, schooling fish that is susceptible to overfishing. In theory, the last school could economically be taken. Also the great year-to-year fluctuation in spawning success makes it difficult to determine an amount that can be safely harvested.

Annual surveys of larvae and, more recently, estimates of egg production, have yielded annual estimates of the anchovy spawning biomass. A reduction fishery is allowed only if the spawning biomass exceeds 1,000,000 tons and then only one-third of the excess may be harvested for reduction. Scientists feel that this conservative approach can protect the resource while allowing a sizable harvest in most years.

Two factors have caused the California Fish and Game Commission to set quotas more conservative than those established by the Pacific Fisheries Management Council. Sportfishermen and environmental groups have long felt that the commercial fishery should be reduced or eliminated. They feel that the anchovy is more valuable as forage for gamefish, commercial fish, pelicans, and marine mammals. They also feel that an intensive commercial anchovy fishery will adversely impact the inshore anchovy live bait fishery that is critical to the huge recreational fishing industry. Area closures (primarily inshore) and reduced quotas have resulted from the concerns expressed by recreational anglers and environmental groups.

A second reason for conservative quotas is the rapid development of the Mexican anchovy fishery. Since 1980, Mexicans fishing on the same anchovy population have increased their landings from 5 to over 300,000 tons annually. The Mexican landings alone often exceed the total allowable catch for the entire central stock of anchovy.

In many years, the anchovy fleet has not come near landing their quota for economic reasons rather than resource availability. The price for anchovies is strongly tied to the price of other high protein feed sources such as soybeans or other souces of fish meal (Peruvian anchoveta or U.S. menhaden). When the price is low the California fishermen will enter other fisheries or stay tied up.

The future of the valuable anchovy fishery depends on how these difficult management problems are resolved. Some form of joint management by Mexico and the United States is essential. Spawning biomass estimates need to be refined and allocation of the resource between the reduction fishery, bait fishery, and forage needs of marine organisms must be resolved.

TROUT AND SALMON
Family Salmonidae

Life History

When one thinks of Pacific Coast fishes, the salmonids come to mind immediately. They are prized for their beauty, commercial value, food value, sportiness, and value as an indicator of the health of the environment. Because this is a book on marine fishes, only those salmonid species that spend part of their life at sea will be discussed.

Five species of salmon inhabit the Pacific Coast of the U.S. They are all of the genus *Oncorhynchus*, which refers to the hooked jaws the males develop when they mature at spawning time. The salmon are all anadromous. Unlike trout, all salmon die after spawning. The salmon return to their home stream to spawn. Therefore, each stream has a stock of salmon that may be uniquely adapted to the conditions of that stream. Large streams, such as the Columbia River, have several "runs" of several species.

The pink salmon, *Oncorhynchus gorbuscha*, is the smallest and most abundant of the five species. They average about 4.5 lb with a maximum size of 12 lb. Pink salmon range from California to Japan, but they are most common in British Columbia and southeastern Alaska. Pink salmon, also known as humpbacks because of the large hump on the back of spawning males, enter streams to spawn during the fall. Approximately 1,500 to 2,000 eggs are laid. The young emerge from the gravel in the spring and migrate to sea by summer. They grow quickly at sea and begin their return migration during their second summer. The pinks are the shortest-lived salmon, living only 2 years. Unlike other salmon who return several age classes of fish to the streams each year, "humpies" are almost always 2-year olds. Thus, there are genetically separate year classes. Currently, the fish returning in odd-numbered years are larger and more numerous than those returning in even-numbered years.

The sockeye or red salmon, *Oncorhynchus nerka*, is highly prized commercially in Canada and Alaska. They are found in commercial quantities from the Columbia River to Bristol Bay, Alaska. Like the pink salmon, sockeye average about 5 lb. They grow to over 33 inches in length. Sockeye are most common in river systems that are connected to lakes. The mature fish spawn far upstream or in springs along the lakes' shores. An average 3,700 eggs are laid. The young sockeye spend 1 or 2 years in fresh water, often in nursery lakes. Growth is often slow and the fish are only 2 to 5 inches long when they migrate to sea. Sockeye spend 1 to 4 years at sea (usually 2 years) before returning to their birthplace to spawn. Landlocked populations of sockeye are known as kokanee salmon.

Oncorhynchus keta, the chum or dog salmon, is most common from Oregon to Alaska. They grow to 33 lb but average about 10 lb at maturity. Chums spawn later than all other salmon; some don't spawn until early spring after entering the stream the previous fall. They tend to spawn at the lower ends of streams, where they lay approximately 3,000 eggs. The young migrate quickly to sea after hatching. Aquaculturists, especially in Japan and Russia, have undertaken massive rearing programs with this species because of the short time required in the hatchery before the fish can go to sea. Chum salmon spend 3 to 5 years at sea and make long feeding migrations. They feed primarily on invertebrates, which makes them less susceptible to trolling gear. Their flesh is usually lighter than other salmon, which results in a lower price paid to fishermen.

The coho or silver salmon, *Oncorhynchus kisutch*, ranges from central California to Alaska. They grow to 30 lb and average about 9 lb at maturity. Coho lay about 4,000 eggs; the young stay in the stream at least 1 year. They are often found in relatively small coastal streams. They remain at sea for 1 to 3 years before returning to spawn and die.

The king or chinook salmon, *Oncorhynchus tshawytscha*, may grow as large as 120 lb. The average size at maturity is between 15 and 30 lb. This species predominates in the Caifornia fishery but is common all the way to Alaska. The time of the spawning run varies from river to river, and there are distinct runs within the largest rivers. Females produce about 5,000 eggs. The young usually go to sea in their first year, where they feed on fish and invertebrates in water deeper than those inhabited by other salmon species. They will stay at sea for 2 to 8 years. The more northerly populations tend to stay at sea long. Because they command a high price, chinook salmon are the object of an intense fishery.

Several species of sea-run trout are common. These are rainbow trout (steelhead), coastal cutthroat trout, and Dolly Varden. Unlike salmon, these fish often survive to go to sea again after spawning. They generally migrate upstream in fall or winter. The young stay in fresh water for 2 or 3 years before going to sea. They may spawn several times. Steelhead often make long migrations at sea, while cutthroat and Dolly Varden tend to remain closer to their home steam.

Fishery Information

Salmon are the most valuable north Pacific fishery; in 1981 fishermen received $438 million for their catch. Historically, the fishery has been, and continues to be, important to Native Americans. In the 1850s canneries began processing salmon netted out of the Sacramento River. Over the next few decades the canneries spread northward toward Alaska. By the 1880s the salmon canning business peaked in the Sacramento and Columbia rivers. Reduced abundance due to heavy fishing and habitat degradation made the canneries uneconomical. In the 20th century the canning industry has operated primarily in Alaska, where sockeye, chum, and pink salmon are most abundant.

Salmon are caught with gillnets, purse seines, traps, and hook and line. The river fishermen used primarily gillnets and fish traps. Both of these gear types are extremely efficient and their use, if not regulated, has led to over-harvesting. As the numbers of fish returning to the rivers declined, fishermen started to go to sea to catch salmon. The use of trolling gear evolved as gasoline engines became common. Lures and baited hooks are trolled at 1 to 3 knots by vessels ranging from 15 to 90 ft. Although this method is relatively inefficient,

it results in a high-quality, high-priced product. Trolling is the only method allowed in California's salmon fishery. In more northerly waters fishermen use seines and gillnets. Seiners harvest salmon as they near their spawning streams by encircling the schools. Gillnets have been used on the high seas by Japanese fishermen to intercept fish from both Japanese and North American streams.

Salmon are also a prized recreational fish. Most are captured at sea by trolling and mooching with bait and lures. Others are caught by anglers using flies, lures, and roe after they enter streams to spawn.

Management of the salmon fishery is highly complex. Many salmon stocks (particulary coho and chinook) have declined significantly in abundance since the early 1900s. This is due largely to habitat degradation caused by water diversions, dams, and poor land management. Hatcheries have helped slow this decline, but they have reversed this trend in only a few cases. As the resource abundance has declined, the value of salmon has risen and attracted large numbers of fishermen. Management agencies are currently struggling with the difficult task of restoring salmon runs and allocating the reduced resource among the numerous diverse user groups who depend on salmon for their livelihood or pleasure.

The rearing of salmon has become important in recent years. Numerous hatcheries, constructed to mitigate for lost spawning grounds, have helped sustain the salmon fishery. In recent years ocean ranching of salmon by private industry has become a controversial reality. Ocean ranchers rear young salmon in a hatchery to achieve higher survivial and faster growth than found in the wild, release the fish to "graze" at sea and then harvest and sell the adults when they return to spawn. Japan and Russia are currently involved in large scale ocean ranching programs. In the United States ocean ranching has developed slowly because of questions about the impacts on the current fishery, concerns about adverse impacts on wild stocks, and doubt about the economic viability of this type of business.

Consumer Information

Salmon is a highly esteemed food. It can be prepared with almost any method. It is commonly smoked, barbecued, poached, fried, or baked. Salmon is often served chilled because of its distinctive flavor and color.

Salmon are moderately oily, so they don't freeze well for long time periods (more than 3 months). Salmon steaks should be frozen in water-filled milk cartons to minimize any contact with air. Of the salmon, chum is the least oily (4%), while chinook has the highest oil content (11.5%).

Salmon is available to the consumer in many different forms from many sources throughout the year. Fresh chinook and coho salmon captured by trollers at sea is considered to be the highest quality salmon. Although the seasons vary each year, fresh troll-caught salmon is generally available from late April through September. Fresh salmon can be purchased as whole fish, half fish, steaks, or fillets. Whole salmon is the least expensive form to buy.

When salmon return to their native streams, many are captured with nets. Some chinook and coho are captured using this method, but nets are the primary method used to catch sockeye, chum, and pink salmon. Most of these fish, especially in Alaska, are canned. Part of these net-caught fish are sold whole at relatively low prices, either fresh or frozen. Fish markets in the Seattle area feature whole net-caught fish most months of the year.

Smoked salmon, including lox and kippered salmon, is available all year. In recent years aquaculture (fish farming) has become a significant source of salmon. American fish farmers produce pen-reared, pan-sized salmon as well as mature salmon from ocean ranching operations. Large Atlantic salmon, *Salmo salar*, reared in pens in Scandinavia, are available in some Pacific Coast markets when fresh Pacific salmon is unavailable.

SMELTS
Family Osmeridae

Life History
True smelts have a small dorsal adipose fin opposite the anal fin which is not present in the silversides (Family Atherinidae). Smelts are small, usually less than 10 inches. Some are marine, some anadromous, and others live strictly in fresh water.

The smelts feed primarily on zooplankton and small fish. Several species spawn on beaches, where the fertilized eggs adhere to sand grains. Other species such as the eulachon, *Thaleichthys pacificus*,

run up northwest rivers in large schools to spawn in riffles. Because of their abundance and small size, the smelts are important prey for many fishes, mammals, and birds. The smelts are common from central California to Alaska.

Fishery Information
Sizable commercial and recreational fisheries exist for three smelt species. Surf smelt, *Hypomesus pretiosus*, and night smelt, *Spirinchus starksi*, are captured in A-frame dip nets in the surf during their spawning runs. Surf smelt dominate catches during the day and night smelt are captured at night. Landings of these two species in California alone usually exceed 400,000 lb annually.

The eulachon, also known as candlefish because of its oily flesh, is abundant in large northwestern rivers such as the Columbia and Fraser. At least 1,000,000 lb are landed each year using dip nets, gillnets, and small trawls. Fishermen take advantage of the massive spawning aggregations to make large catches.

Consumer Information
Surf and night smelt are very delicate and have a sweet flavor when properly prepared. Most people head and gut the smelt soon after capture or purchase. Frying is the preferred preparation method.

The eulachon is quite oily. They used to be dried, threaded with a wick, and used as candles. The oiliness makes this smelt species difficult to store. Most anglers smoke their eulachon catch.

Whole fresh smelt are available in coastal fish markets from late spring through fall when they are landed by local commercial fishermen. Fresh smelt are uncommon in markets south of San Francisco. Frozen, headed, and gutted smelt from the Great Lakes are occasionally available in Pacific Coast markets.

CODFISHES (HAKE)
Family Gadidae

Life History
Pacific Hake, *Merluccius productus*, also called Pacific whiting, is one of the most important fishes in the coastal marine ecosystems off California, Oregon, and Washington. Population estimates as high

as 400,000 metric tons (880 million lb) have been made by the National Marine Fisheries Service. Hake are an important predator on invertebrates while serving as prey for larger fish.

Hake occur from the Gulf of California and southern California during the winter. The pelagic eggs hatch and the larvae are able to swim within a few days. Hake live for at least 13 years and grow to 31 inches.

Hake are semipelagic. They school near the bottom during the day and then migrate upward in the night, following their prey. They feed primarily on euphausiids. Hake also migrate along the coast. During the spring and summer they move northward and then they move southward during the fall toward their winter spawning grounds.

Fishery Information

An active commercial hake fishery has existed since 1966 in California, Oregon, and Washington. Fishermen had long been aware of the huge resource because they often caught large amounts of hake in bottom trawls. The hake were always discarded or used for animal feed because there was no market in the United States for them.

In 1966 large Russian trawlers began catching hake off the Pacific Coast, using sophisticated midwater trawls and electronic fish finding equipment. By 1970, several other nations had entered the fishery and huge landings were made. The large foreign vessels were equipped with processing equipment which allowed them to process the hake within 4 hr and then freeze it. This quick processing is essential for hake because 20 to 40% of them are infested with a microscopic parasite which secretes an enzyme that softens the flesh soon after the fish dies. Few American fishermen were equipped with midwater trawls and the equipment to process large quantities of hake on board during the 1960s and 1970s. The only domestic hake fishery was a brief one for fish protein concentrate during the late 1960s.

A dramatic change occurred in 1976 with the passage of the Fishery Conservation and Management Act establishing a 200-mile fisheries zone. The foreign catch is now regulated by the United States and the foreign fishermen are only permitted to harvest the portion of the allowable catch that is in excess of what the United States fishing industry intends to harvest. This dramatic change encouraged fishing, processing, and marketing ventures by the domestic industry.

Development of a totally domestic hake fishery has been slow due to continued problems with processing, marketing, and low prices. Although a change in the market name to whiting and the development of some institutional and urban markets has helped, most hake is marketed overseas.

Innovative fishermen have adapted to the situation by participating in joint ventures with foreign or partially foreign-owned companies. Fishermen capture the hake in large quantities and immediately off-load the net onto a foreign processing ship. The ship processes the fish while the American vessels continue to fish. Until the domestic fishing industry develops processing capability and markets, joint ventures will be the primary method for American fishermen to harvest a portion of this huge resource. In 1982 it was estimated that 175,000 metric tons (385,000,000 lb) of hake could be taken without damaging the population. This is more than the combined bottomfish catch of California, Oregon, and Washington.

Consumer Information

Hake are known to the consumer as whiting. Several whiting species are abundant in other temperate waters of the world. Whiting is usually marketed as fillets or in a headed and gutted form. The price is usually relatively low.

Fresh Pacific whiting is available during the spring and summer months as fillets or headed and gutted. During the rest of the year, frozen Pacific whiting or headed and gutted whiting from other parts of the world can be purchased. As the U. S. whiting fishery develops, we may see whiting in prepared products such as fish patties.

Whiting has a very delicate texture and mild flavor. They are relatively low in fat. The microscopic parasite is not a health hazard; it just makes the flesh very mushy if the fish is not chilled and processed rapidly. The most successful preparation method is deep-fat frying because it results in the best texture. Experiments are being conducted to test the use of hake in baked dishes with sauce, minced products, and hot dogs. Eventually this large resource will be used by Americans in significant quantities.

FLYINGFISHES
Family Exocoetidae

Life History

One of the most spectacular oceanic fishes is the flyingfish. They use their strong tail to propel themselves out of the water so they can use their huge wing-like pectoral fins for soaring. Their behavior enables them to escape large predators such as marlin and tuna. They can soar for 200 ft at heights up to 50 ft and at speeds exceeding 20 miles per hour.

The California flyingfish, *Cypselurus californicus*, is the world's largest, growing to 18 inches. It is common in southern California where its acrobatics have entertained tourists and boaters around Catalina Island. Spawning occurs during summer months, when hundreds of eggs are attached to floating objects. The eggs hatch in about 2 weeks.

Fishery and Consumer Information

A valuable commercial fishery exists in southern California. The fish are captured with nets for bait. Flyingfish receive high prices as bait for marlin, yellowtail, sailfish, tuna, and swordfish.

Flyingfish are also a good food fish. They can be filleted and fried or broiled. They are quite low in fat. Consumers are most likely to find flying fish in Southern California markets during the summer and fall months.

SILVERSIDES
Family Atherinidae

Life History

Silversides are commonly known as smelt, but they lack the small adipose fin of the true smelt and have two dorsal fins instead of one. Three silversides are found along the Pacific Coast: the jacksmelt, the topsmelt, and the famous grunion.

The jacksmelt, *Atherinopsis californiensis*, is the largest silverside. It is distinguished from the other two species by its bright yellow cheek area and several rows of simple teeth on the jaw. Jacksmelt grow to over 17 inches and range from Baja California to central Oregon. They prefer inshore and estuarine waters, where they feed primarily on small crustaceans in the upper part of the water column. Spawning takes place during the winter, when eggs are attached to eelgrass and kelp.

Grunion, *Leuresthes tenuis*, is the smallest (7 inches) and most unique silverside. They are found from Baja California to Monterey Bay. The grunion is one of the few fish species that spawns on sandy beaches. They ride the waves up onto the beach at night during high tides following a new or full moon during the spring and summer. The females burrow into the sand to lay their eggs which are then fertilized by the males. Several weeks later, during the next series of highest tides, the eggs quickly hatch and are swept out to sea.

Fishery Information

Jacksmelt make up the majority of the commercial catch. When demand was high (1940s) the landings reached 2,000,000 lb. However, the low market demand since then has kept commercial landings below 200,000 lb per year. The fish are captured in nets and by hook and line.

Anglers fishing off rocks and piers catch large numbers of jacksmelt. Because these fish are usually found near the surface, a series of small hooks are suspended under a float. Shrimp, squid, mussels, and anchovies all make good bait. Strings of small, feathered hooks and small shiny lures are also effective. I have seen jacksmelt taken on flies also.

Consumer Information

Topsmelt and grunion are usually pan-fried or broiled utilizing the methods used to prepare true smelts. The larger jacksmelt can be filleted and then fried or broiled. Jacksmelt are most available to consumers during the spring and summer as whole fish.

ROCKFISHES
Family Scorpaenidae

Life History

This large family of fishes is of interest both biologically and economically. Currently, taxonomists list 69 species of rockfish (genus *Sebastes*) along the Pacific Coast. This number seems to grow annually as more is learned about this family. Many *Sebastes* species look similar and occur in similar habitats. The evolution and ecology of this interesting group of fishes has interested many researchers.

In general, rockfishes are slow-growing. A 15-inch rockfish may be 15 years old. Some species appear to live to be well over 30 years old. Rockfishes tend to reach sexual maturity at a late age, usually between 5 and 10 years. Most rockfish are ovovivaparous, which means that fertilization is internal and large numbers of larvae (up to 2,000,000) are released. The larvae are generally released during the winter and the young are found in nearshore waters during the spring. Rockfishes are usually associated with rocks or kelp. The inshore species tend to stay in the same territory while the offshore species appear to migrate more, perhaps in search of food. Comparing rockfishes that occur in different habitat types provides more insight into this diverse group.

The young of several species occur in estuaries during the first 3 or 4 years of life. The copper (*Sebastes caurinus*), brown (*Sebastes auriculatus*) and black (*Sebastes melanops*) rockfish occur in rocky areas and around pilings in large bays. These fish appear to be quite territorial. Several young brown rockfish released in the ocean outside the Golden Gate Bridge quickly found their way back to their capture site well inside San Francisco Bay (over 10 miles away). These young fish will later migrate into deeper offshore waters as they mature.

Another interesting group of rockfish occurs in nearshore rocky kelp beds. The blue, black, and olive rockfish occupy the midwater area, while species such as the gopher and black and yellow rockfish occur near the bottom. The midwater rockfishes may move to offshore reefs at times to feed. The bottom-dwelling species don't migrate and they defend their territories vigorously. Studies of feeding habits, particularly during times when food is scarce, show little overlap in prey, suggesting that these rockfishes are partioning the limited food resource.

Further offshore, the rockfish species tend to be less restricted to a home area. They may need to move around more in search of food which is scarcer offshore. The widow rockfish (*Sebastes entomelas*) and the shortbelly rockfish (*Sebastes jordani*) are two of the most abundant species. They both form dense schools just above the bottom and their foot habits are quite similar. However, the shortbelly disperses at night like most rockfish species, while the widow rockfish form schools at night. Fishermen have used knowledge of this schooling behavior to make large catches.

Ecologists have long wondered why there are so many species of rockfish and how they attain and maintain the reproductive isolation necessary for speciation. Several theories have been suggested, and all of them may contribute to the evolution of these interesting fish. Some researchers feel that speciation occurs at the extremes of the ranges during times of climatic changes (ice ages). Several species appear to have evolved in the Gulf of California when populations became isolated during the Pleistocene glacial periods. Other scientists feel that ocean current patterns have provided the necessary geographic isolation. Some scientists have hypothesized that the difference in current patterns north and south of Point Conception, California, are responsible for some morphological differences in the kelp rockfish, *Sebastes atrovirens*. This may be an example of speciation in progress. Another theory suggests that behavioral mechanisms related to sight and sound have evolved which separate groups for mating. Many rockfish species occur close together and appear quite similar, but there are few hybrids.

In addition to the rockfish of the *Sebastes* genus, there are several other interesting members of the Scorpaenidae family along the Pacific Coast. The thornyheads, genus *Sebastolobus*, occur in relatively deep water. These bright red, commercially important fish are also known as idiot fish or channel rockfish. The sculpin or California scorpionfish, *Scorpaena guttata*, frequents kelp beds and rocky areas in southern California. This colorful fish is best known for the virulent vernom in its spines. If one is stuck by the spines, it can be intensely painful.

Fishery Information

Rockfish are one of the most important fishery resources for both recreational and commercial fishermen. In recent years rockfish have been the leading sportfish in California. It is a year-round fishery that is becoming popular along the entire coast. The key to catching rockfish is find the rocky or kelp bed habitat they prefer. Recording fathometers are helpful in finding a suitable habitat and schools of rockfish. The primary gear used by anglers is a leader with three or four feathered hooks baited with squid, anchovy, or herring. Often 1 or 2 lb of weight is needed to get down to where the fish are concentrated. At times bait is unnecessary and lures such as scampi, plastic worms, or hex-bar jigs are effective. Anglers land about 7,000,000 lb of rockfish annually.

The commercial fishery for rockfish is large and diversified. It varies from skiff fishermen who use hook and line to expensive midwater trawlers that chase widow rockfish. In the early 1980s over 40,000 metric tons of rockfish were landed annually. At least half of this catch was the widow rockfish.

Many types of gear are used to catch rockfish commercially. Rod and reel, longlines, gillnets, and trawls are the primary gear types. Small vessels using rod and reel or longlines often target on nearshore species that are highly desired by some ethnic groups. Gillnets are very effective for catching rockfish, but their use is limited by regulation, by concerns about the incidental catch, and by concerns of recreational anglers that the nets are too effective. Bottom trawlers capture rockfish along with flatfish and other species while some midwater trawlers target directly on widow or shortbelly rockfish.

The widow and shortbelly rockfish occur in dense schools near but off the bottom so they are not very vulnerable to bottom trawls. With the aid of sophisticated electronics, midwater trawlers can locate these schools and pull their nets through the fish. If all goes well, a midwater trawler can land over 100,000 lb in a half-hour set. The development of this technique in the later 1970s resulted in a new fishery landing over 60,000,000 lb of widow rockfish. By 1982 a quota was imposed because of concern about the resource. Densely schooling fish resources are vulnerable to heavy fishing and often give little warning before the population crashes.

As the widow rockfish fishery leveled off and began to decline in the early 1980s, interest grew in the shortbelly rockfish. This small (less than 12 inches long) rockfish exists in huge quantities off central California. Until markets and United States' processing capability expands, this resource will be harvested primarily by joint ventures with other nations. There is some concern about harvesting shortbelly rockfish because it is an important forage species for salmon during some months.

Consumer Information

If fishery biologists have a difficult time identifying the scores of rockfish species, then consumers will find it nearly impossible. A group of 15 common species are marketed as Pacific red snapper. While this is a good marketing name, it has upset the fishing industry in the Gulf of Mexico where they land the true red snapper (family Lutjanidae). To add to the confusion, Pacific Coast rockfish are also marketed as rock cod, snapper, and ocean perch. My suggestion is to not worry about the name, just learn to recognize good quality fish.

Rockfish have a firm texture that lends itself well to most preparation methods. Rockfish are most commonly sold as fillets or whole fish. They are generally one of the most economically priced fish. Rockfish are available fresh and frozen all year. Whole fish can be a bargain because one can get more meat off of a fish cooked whole. Those who want to buy whole rockfish to fillet themselves should remember that they will get about a 30% yield as fillets.

Many small-scale commercial fishermen are beginning to hook and line fish for rockfish on a daily basis. This make high quality whole rockfish available. Fish markets in large urban areas (Seattle, San Francisco) and markets in fish ports (e.g. Monterey, Santa Cruz) sell fresh whole rockfish. The important species in the south include the bocaccio, chilipepper, brown, and blue rockfishes. As one moves northward the black, canary, yellowtail, and copper rockfish become more prevalent.

Worms are often found in rockfish flesh. These worms are harmless if thoroughly cooked. Rockfish generally should not be eaten raw.

Rockfish are high in protein (19 gm/100gm) and low in fat (1 gm/100 gm).

Print 1   Northern California Kelp Bed Fishes

Print 2   Brown Smoothhound   *Mustelus henlei*

Print 3   Big Skate   *Raja binoculata*

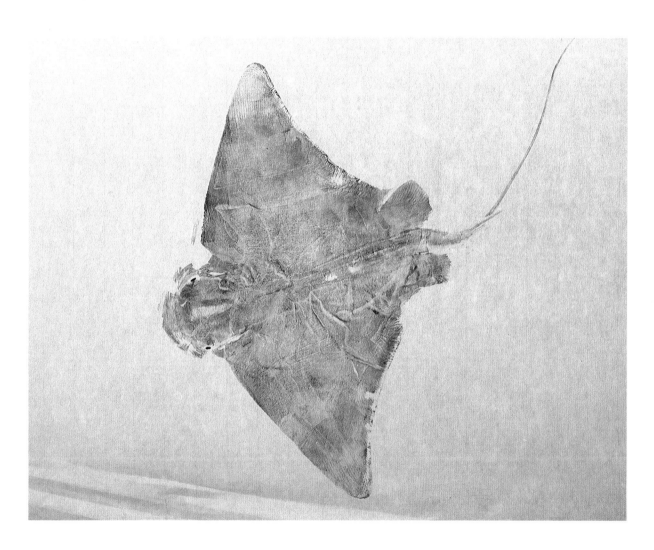

Print 4   Bat Ray   *Myliobatus californica*

Print 5 White Sturgeon *Acipenser transmontanus*

Print 6   American Shad   *Alosa sapidissima*

Print 7   Pacific Herring   *Clupea harengus pallasi*

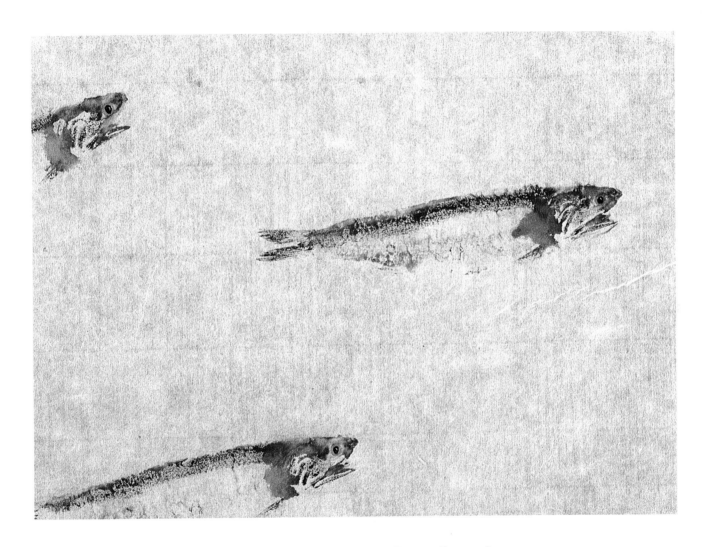

Print 8   Northern Anchovy   *Engraulis mordax*

Print 9   Chinook Salmon   *Oncorhynchus tshawytscha*

Print 10   Coho Salmon   *Oncorhynchus kisutch*

Print 11   Steelhead   *Salmo gairdneri*

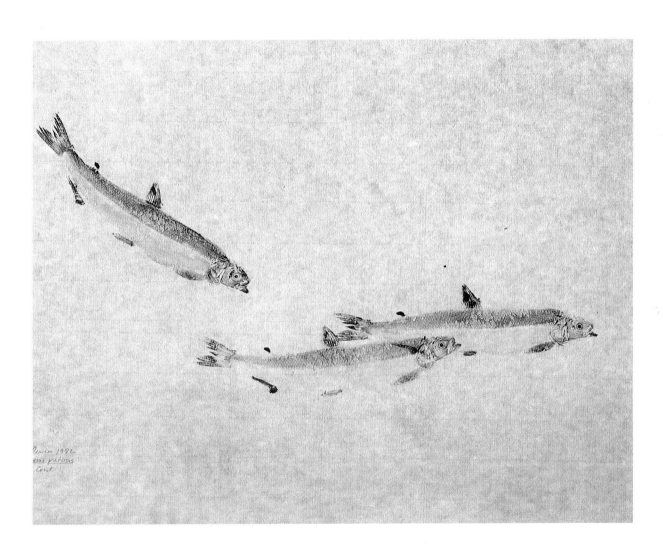

Print 12   Surf Smelt   _Hypomesus pretiosus_

Print 13   Pacific Hake   *Merluccius productus*

Print 14   California Flyingfish   *Cypselurus californicus*

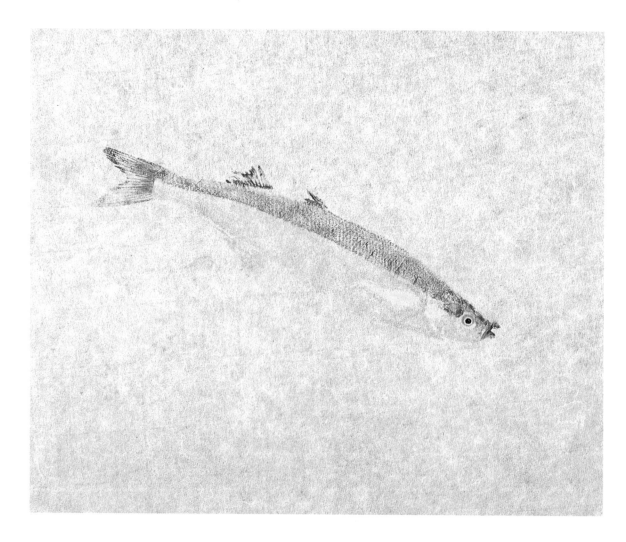

Print 15   Jacksmelt   *Atherinopsis californiensis*

Print 16   California Scorpionfish   *Scorpaena guttata*

Print 17   Gopher Rockfish   _Sebastes carnatus_

Print 18 Brown Rockfish *Sebastes auriculatus*

Print 19   Blue Rockfish   *Sebastes mystinus*

Print 20   Widow Rockfish   *Sebastes entomelas*

Print 21   Rosy Rockfish   *Sebastes rosaceus*

Christopher M. Dewees 1980
redbanded rockfish
Sebastes babcocki
Shelter Cove, Ca.

Print 22   Redbanded Rockfish   *Sebastes babcocki*

Print 23   Greenstriped Rockfish   *Sebastes elongatus*

Print 24   Canary Rockfish   *Sebastes pinniger*

Print 25   China Rockfish   *Sebastes nebulosus*

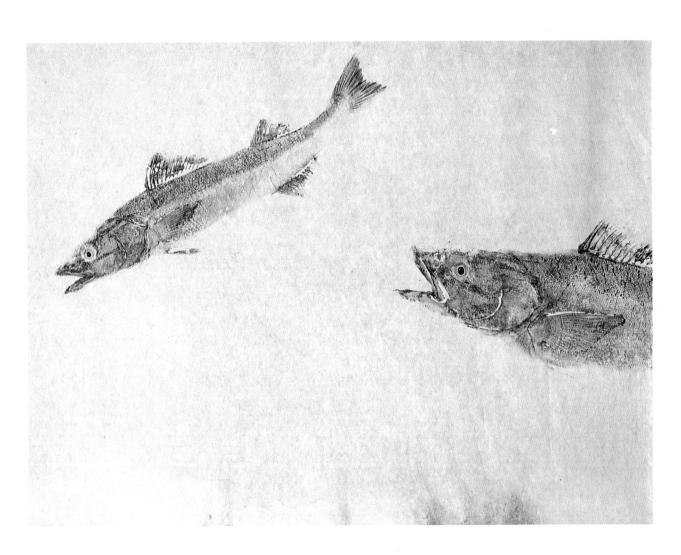

Print 26 Sablefish *Anoplopoma fimbria*

Print 27 Lingcod *Ophiodon elongatus*

Print 28   Kelp Greenling   *Hexagrammos decagrammus*

Print 29   Cabezon   *Scorpaenichthys marmoratus*

Print 30   Pacific Staghorn Sculpin   *Leptocottus armatus*

Print 31   Lavender Sculpin   *Leiocottus hirundo*

SABLEFISHES
Family Anoplopomatidae

Life History

The sablefish, *Anoplopoma fimbria*, is the most abundant representative of the family Anoplopomatidae along the U.S. Pacific Coast. The sablefish is also known as blackcod to the fishing industry and as butterfish in filleted form to the consumer. The sablefish is one of the dominant demersal fish along the continental slope at depths greater than 1,200 ft.

Muddy bottoms in or near submarine canyons are the principal habitat for sablefish. They range from Baja California north to the Bering Sea and southwest to the Japanese coast. Sablefish are most abundant at depths greater than 200 fathoms; peak abundance occurs at greater depths as one moves southward.

Sablefish males and females begin spawning at 5 and 7 years of age, respectively, during the winter months. Females produce 100,000 to 1,000,000 eggs; few survive to maturity. Sablefish are opportunistic feeders, feeding on fish and crustaceans. Some sablefish live at least 20 years and reach a maximum size of 40 inches.

Fishery Information

Historically, Pacific Coast Indians caught sablefish. A sizeable commercial fishery didn't develop until World War II. In the 1960s and early 1970s Japan, Russia, Korea, and Taiwan captured well over 100,000,000 lb annually. In recent years the U.S. sablefish landings have varied widely because of a very erratic export market. Trawls, longlines, and large traps (3 ft x 3 ft x 8 ft) are used to capture sablefish in all of the Pacific Coast states.

Consumer Information

Oiliness is the most outstanding characteristic of sablefish flesh. Sablefish has a fat content of about 14% compared with 11.5% in the chinook salmon. The high oil content makes sablefish excellent for smoking. The majority of sablefish is smoked. Consumers along the Pacific Coast can find sablefish year around. Most common is the filleted form, usually called butterfish in seafood markets. Whole sablefish can be obtained through seafood markets for home smoking or use in Scandanavian-style recipes. Smoked or kippered sablefish is often marketed as "kippered Alaskan cod."

LINGCOD AND GREENLINGS
Family Hexagrammidae

Life History

The Hexagrammidae is a relatively small family represented by about 10 species along the Pacific Coast. They are generally recognized by their elongated bodies, a long, deeply notched dorsal fin, and multiple lateral lines on some species. Except for the lingcod, they all inhabit nearshore, shallow waters.

The greenlings live on shallow reefs and in subtidal rocky areas along the coast. They are distinguished from the rest of this family by four or five lateral lines on each side of their body. Greenlings are primarily bottom dwellers that feed on invertebrates common in subtidal areas. They spawn during the winter and the young are often found well offshore, especially in the Gulf of Alaska. All species of greenling are beautifully colored. Their coloration varies seasonally and is different between sexes of several greenlings. For example, the female kelp greenling, *Hexagrammos decagrammus*, is usually brownish with numerous round, orange spots. The male is often greyish with bright blue spots on the head and front half of the body. The kelp greenling is the largest species, growing to 21 inches. The painted greenling is the smallest, rarely over 6 inches long.

Lingcod, *Ophiodon elongatus*, range along the entire Pacific Coast. They grow to a length of 5 ft and a weight of 105 lb. They are voracious predators on other fish and shellfish such as herring, rockfish, octopus, flatfish, greenling, and squid. Adult lingcod are residents of reefs at depths from a few feet to 1,400 ft. The young spend their first year or two on sandy bottoms, where they are probably avoiding predation by their older siblings. There is evidence that at least a portion of the adult population migrates from offshore reefs to subtidal areas for winter spawning. Females attach large masses of eggs (up to 500,000) to rocks. The males fertilize the eggs and guard the egg masses during the 1- to 2-month incubation period. The young grow rapidly and all are sexually mature at 4 years (20-inch males) and 7 years (30-inch females).

Fishery Information

Greenlings are primarily a recreational fish. Most catches are made on rocky shores by anglers using mussels, squid, anchovies, and shrimp as bait. They are often found in areas of heavy kelp, where they feed on invertebrates associated with the plants. Live greenling make excellent lingcod bait.

Lingcod are of major importance to both the recreational and commercial fisheries along the entire coast. Although populations are holding up well, there is concern about overfishing on lingcod stocks in some areas, such as Puget Sound.

The U.S. commercial fishery currently lands about 7,500,000 lb annually. Most of this is landed by trawlers as an incidental catch. A significant amount is also captured by hook and line and longline.

Consumer Information

Both greenlings and lingcod are excellent eating. The greenlings have a very fine, delicate texture that is best when cooked quickly. Lingcod tend to be coarser but fine-flavored fish. Lingcod are usually marketed as fillets, but are also available whole and steaked. Lingcod are available throughout the year. They are excellent broiled or baked. Lingcod are very low in fat, less than 1 gm per 100 gm.

Some greenlings and lingcod have a blue or green tinge to their flesh which concerns consumers. This color is harmless and doesn't affect quality. As soon as the flesh is cooked, it turns white. The coloration may be related to the fishes' diet.

SCULPINS
Family Cottidae

Life History

Over 50 species of sculpins are found in Pacific marine waters. Other species are important in fresh water. Most members of the family are small, dwelling on the bottom in waters of less than 100 ft. The sculpins are most obvious in tidepools.

The cottids tend to have large heads and large pectoral fins that are used to support themselves and to move around. They have few or no scales and two dorsal fins.

Two of the larger species, the Pacific staghorn sculpin, *Leptocottus armatus*, and the cabezon, *Scorpaenichthys marmoratus*, have been studied in detail. The staghorn sculpin is probably the most common cottid. It occurs primarily in bays, although it is often found well up

coastal streams. They are short-lived; fish over 3 years old are rare. Staghorn sculpins spawn during the winter months, laying up to 11,000 eggs. They feed on amphipods, bay shrimp, worms, and small fish. They are preyed upon by striped bass, other large fishes, and birds.

The cabezon grows to 25 lb, making it the largest cottid. They are found from tidepools to depths of 250 ft. They spawn during the winter, laying egg masses containing up to 100,000 eggs in a nest guarded by the male. Cabezon grow to 18 inches within 3 years and are ferocious predators. Crabs, abalone, and small fishes are common victims. The cabezon's large, powerful mouth makes it effective at feeding on invertebrates attached to rocks or algae.

Most other sculpins are less than 10 inches long. Many of them live in rocky intertidal and subtidal habitats, where their protective coloration makes them practically invisible until they move.

Fishery Information

The sculpins are of little importance to commercial and recreational fisheries. The only species with current economic value is the cabezon. It is prized by anglers fishing rocky shores, primarily in California. Although they can be captured with many baits, I've had most success with abalone trimmings fished during an incoming tide when the cabezon come into the intertidal zone to feed. Cabezon are caught incidentally by commercial hook and line fishermen. Commercial landings are usually less than 20,000 lb annually.

There is a minor fishery for staghorn sculpins for use as striped bass bait in San Francisco Bay. Large stripers are captured, primarily during the winter months, using whole sculpins.

Consumer Information

The only species consumed in significant quantity is the cabezon. The flesh, like the lingcod's, often has a greenish tint. This coloration is harmless and disappears when the fish is cooked. The cabezon is exceptional among Pacific Coast fishes because it has poisonous eggs (roe). I remember being very impressed as a child by an adventuresome biologist's vivid report of being violently ill after eating cabezon roe.

Cabezon are available in small quantities throughout the year to consumers because they are an incidental catch taken by rockfish fishermen. Cabezon are usually marketed whole.

SEA BASSES
Family Serranidae

Life History

This large family has over 400 species worldwide, mostly in tropical waters. Ten species occur along the Pacific Coast. The best known are the stripped bass and the kelp bass. All are carniverous and highly esteemed by fishermen.

The striped bass, *Morone saxatilis*, is native to the Atlantic Coast. In 1879 and 1882, 432 fish were brought west in milk cans by train and released in the San Francisco Bay area. Within a decade, the population was large enough to support a commercial fishery. Striped bass are anadromous. When they spawn in the spring, the females release semi-buoyant eggs that need adequate water flow to keep them off of the bottom. After the eggs hatch, the young feed on small crustaceans in the lower parts of the river systems. The variables affecting survivial of the young in the San Francisco Bay area are not fully understood, but water flows, food supply, and predation may all be important. Striped bass that survive their first 2 years feed heavily on small fish in bays and along ocean beaches. Stripers grow to a maximum size of 4 ft and 90 lb. They range from southern California to British Columbia, but are most common around San Francisco Bay.

Kelp bass, *Paralabrax clathratus*, are primarily southern California residents. They are found in nearshore waters at depths of less than 200 ft and are closely associated with kelp beds and rocks. They appear to be non-migratory and feed on small fish and invertebrates throughout the kelp canopy. They are an important part of kelp bed fish communities. Kelp bass grow to 28 inches and 14 lb.

Fishery Information

Historically, the basses have been important commercially. However, their extreme value as sportfish has led California to allocate basses primarily to the recreational fishery.

A sizable commercial fishery existed for striped bass in San Francisco Bay until 1935. Sportfishermen now take them with lures and live or dead anchovies, perch, staghorn sculpins, grass shrimp, worms, and threadfin shad. Populations have declined drastically from 4.5 to 1.2 million fish since 1960; the catch has also declined. Reasons for this decline are still poorly understood. Reduced water flows, water diversions, parasites, and the sublethal effects of pollutants are among the possible causes. While in-depth research continues, bag and size limits have been changed to offer more protection to the resource. Aquaculture techniques offer some hope for enhancement and the development of a commercial pond culture industry.

The kelp bass commercial fishery usually landed less than 300,000 lb until it was banned in 1953. The recreational fishery catch has often exceeded 7,500,000 fish annually. In recent years declining catches have led to a 12-inch minimum size limit and a smaller bag limit to allow the fish a chance to spawn at least once.

Kelp bass are often captured with live bait. Fishermen also have success with squid, lures, or plastic worms. These bass tend to feed in the evening and early morning hours and that is the best time to fish for them.

Consumer Information

The sea basses are highly esteemed as food. They are generally lean (1.5 gm of fat per 100 gm) and mild-flavored. Most common fish preparation methods work well and they are excellent when smoked.

Much of the fish marketed as sea bass is actually a large croaker, called white sea bass. This fish will be discussed in the chapter on croakers. Small amounts of true sea bass are available the year around to consumers. Much of this is imported from Mexico. Striped bass from the commercial fishery in the Atlantic and from aquaculture operations is sold whole. These fish are specially identified with tags to prevent the illegal sale of sport-caught striped bass. Striped bass is most common in markets during the summer and fall months.

JACKS
Family Carangidae

Life History

The jacks are generally fast-swimming fish that are good food fish. Two species, the yellowtail, *Seriola lalandei*, and the jack mackerel, *Trachurus symmetricus*, are common off the Pacific Coast.

The yellowtail is most common south of Santa Barbara. Its population is centered off Baja California and schools of them appear off San Diego and the Channel Islands during the summer. Yellowtail mature by the time they are 3 years old, when they are about 1 ft long.

Large females will lay close to 1,000,000 eggs. Yellowtail feed on anchovies, squid, pelagic crabs, mackerel, and other fishes. They grow to 5 ft long and weigh up to 80 lb.

Jack mackerel are distributed along the entire coast. It appears that the smaller fish are found inshore in the south, while larger fish occur further offshore and to the north. Jack mackerel grow rapidly to 10 inches and become sexually mature in their first 2 years. They appear to spawn offshore. They feed on copepods, euphausiids, young squid, and anchovies. Jack mackerel serve as prey for large fishes. They grow to 32 inches long and live for over 25 years. They appear to migrate northward in the summer months.

Fishery Information

The brightly colored, powerful, fast-swimming yellowtail is a highly esteemed sportfish in southern California. The commercial fishery landed 3 to 10,000,000 lb annually until the canneries stopped processing it in the 1950s. Since then, annual commercial landings have usually been less than 1,000,000 lb. The recreational fishery is centered in San Diego where live squid, anchovies, and lures are used to take yellowtail near islands and kelp beds. The annual catch is less than 40,000 fish except during warm water years (e.g. 1957-1960), when hundreds of thousands are captured.

Unlike the yellowtail, the relatively sluggish and drab jack mackerel is not a famous sportfish. The commercial fishery was minor until the late 1940s when the decline of sardine and Pacific mackerel catches and the dropping of the name "horse mackerel" increased demand. Catches have ranged between 10,000 and 66,000 tons since then. Most of the landings come from the Los Angeles area, where purse seines and lampara nets are used.

The recreational catch varies widely. When large jack mackerel are available in southern California, anglers use live anchovies to catch them. Most catches along the rest of the West Coast occur incidentally while salmon fishing.

Consumer Information

Yellowtail and jack mackerel are both good food fish, although the yellowtail are more highly esteemed. Both fish benefit from immediate bleeding after they are captured. They are good broiled, barbecued, or smoked.

The majority of the commercial jack mackerel catch is canned for either human consumption or pet food. Small whole mackerel are sometimes marketed fresh. Yellowtail is usually marketed fresh during the summer months either filleted or whole. Fresh jack mackerel and yellowtail are uncommon in markets north of California.

POMFRETS
Family Bramidae

Life History

Five species of this little-studied family occur off the Pacific Coast. The most abundant is probably the Pacific pomfret, *Brama japonica*. They occur throughout the north Pacific, primarily in offshore waters. Pacific pomfret live primarily in surface waters, where they feed on squid, fish, and crustaceans. They have been found in waters between 50° and 66° F, seeming to prefer waters of 50° to 57° F. They grow to 4 ft in length, but most catches consist of 12 to 18-inch fish.

Pomfret appear to be quite abundant in the north Pacific. Salmon and pomfret are seldom found together in large numbers. Pomfret tend to prefer waters slightly warmer than those preferred by salmon, thus "avoiding" competition for prey. As the surface waters cool in the winter, pomfret migrate southward. In the summer they head into the Gulf of Alaska.

Fishery Information

No directed fishery exists for this species. Incidental catches by the Japanese salmon gillnetters on the high seas indicate that very large populations may exist in the Gulf of Alaska. Pomfret have also been captured accidently in purse seines and by albacore trollers.

The National Marine Fisheries Service (NMFS) feels that *Brama japonica* is one of the largest underutilized fish resources in the north Pacific. Because there is no U.S. high seas gillnet fishery, little is known about the distribution and behavior of this species. Perhaps some of the many commercial fishermen searching for alternatives to traditional fisheries will begin experimentally fishing this resource. Large vessels (50 ft and longer) will be needed to exploit this high seas resource. Pomfret should eventually bring a good market price. More research is needed on pomfret biology, population dynamics, and fishing methods.

Consumer Information

Pomfret is an excellent food fish. We used to often eat a similar pomfret species in Chile. NMFS studies on *Brama japonica* show that it is high in protein (22-23%) and low in fat. It is excellent when prepared by all common fish cooking methods. Pomfret is rarely seen in Pacific Coast seafood markets.

DRUMS
Family Sciaenidae

Life History

The 10 northeastern Pacific species of this family are found primarily in waters south of northern California, although the white croaker and white sea bass are occasionally found off Oregon and Alaska. Members of this family are found primarily in nearshore warm waters over sandy bottoms. They are called croakers because they can vibrate their gas bladder to produce loud sounds. It is believed that these sounds serve some function during spawning.

The white seabass, *Atractoscion nobilis*, is the largest Pacific Coast croaker; it reaches 90 lb. They spawn in the late spring and the eggs are pelagic. Males mature at 20 inches and females at about 24 inches. They apparently migrate in the spring northward from Mexican waters to spawn. They are more of a midwater fish than most croakers; they actively chase and eat squid, pelagic red crabs, and various fish throughout the water column.

The white croaker, *Genyonemus lineatus*, is more typical of small, demersal croakers. This fish is extremely common south of San Francisco. Large schools are common in nearshore waters less than 100 ft deep. At times they are abundant in bays and along beaches. White croakers reach maturity when they are about 6 inches long (2 or 3 years old). They feed on numerous inshore invertebrates and small fish. White croakers are eaten by large fishes and marine mammals. They reach about 16 inches in length.

Fishery Information

Most members of the family Sciaenidae are important fishery resources.

White sea bass have always been highly esteemed as a food fish. The fishery grew rapidly from 250,000 lb in 1889 to 2,500,000 lb in the early 1920s. Later the catches leveled off at about 1,300,000 lb. In recent years the catch has continued to decline and strict size, gear, and season restrictions have been implemented to protect the resource. Catches are usually highest during warm water years when more sea bass remain in California waters.

Commercial fishermen catch white sea bass primarily with gill nets set just outside of kelp beds in southern California. Some are also captured by hook and line. Recreational fishermen use live squid and anchovies to catch the prized sea bass.

The small white croaker is not a high-prized trophy fish like its relative, the white sea bass. It is often called tomcod or kingfish. Its abundance makes it economically important. White croakers often are near the top in numbers in the sportfishing catch. They are captured off piers in great numbers using small hooks baited with squid, worms, or anchovies. The commercial fishery has grown to well over 1,000,000 lb in recent years. Much of the fishing growth is due to in-increased effort by Indo-Chinese immigrants using gillnets in nearshore waters.

Many other croakers are prized by sportsmen because of their fighting and eating qualities. Most of them are captured in the surf and off piers along sandy beaches. Common baits such as pile worms, crabs, mussels, and shrimp work well. Many croakers feed heavily at night and are most vulnerable to fishermen at that time. Two species of croaker, the orangemouth corvina and the bairdiella, were successfully introduced into the Salton Sea in the early 1950s. The orangemouth corvina is now the object of a large sportfishery.

Consumer Information

Sciaenid fishes are highly prized food fishes. They are generally a lean fish that is best baked or broiled. The white croaker is often discarded by recreational fishermen because it is considered to be soft-fleshed and worm-infested. If properly handled, quickly gutted and chilled, the white croaker is a good food fish. Occasional worms found in white croakers and many other marine fishes are completely harmless if the flesh is thoroughly cooked.

White sea bass and white croakers are the primary croakers marketed. These species are available primarily in California markets because that is where this small fishery is centered. Most white sea bass is marketed filleted and is not available during the closed season in the spring. White croakers are available all year in whole form. Markets serving oriental or southeast Asian customers are the best places to look for white croaker.

SEA CHUBS
Family Kyphosidae

Life History
This family is found primarily on tropical reefs, but three species are found in southern California. The opaleye, *Girella nigricans*, and and the halfmoon, *Medialuna californiensis*, are the most common.

The opaleye is identified by its bright blue eyes, green body, and one or two distinctive white spots under the dorsal fin. They spawn in the spring and the eggs and larvae are pelagic. They reach a maximum size of 25 inches and 13 lb. They feed on both algae and encrusting invertebrates.

The halfmoon is identified by a half-moon shaped tail and dark blue dorsal shading. They spawn during the summer and the pelagic larvae eventually settle out around kelp beds. They grow to 19 inches and 5 lb. Like the opaleye, they feed on algae and encrusting organisms. Their diet appears to be less vegetarian than that of the opaleye.

Fishery and Consumer Information
This family is captured primarily by sport fishermen along the southern California coast and the Channel Islands. Opaleye are often a challenge to catch and fishermen have developed specialized techniques using small hooks baited with green, moss-like algae and green peas. They occasionally are caught on more traditional baits. Mussels and shrimp are the best baits for halfmoon. A minor commercial fishery exists for these species which are often marketed as "perch" or "Catalina blue perch" (halfmoon).

Both of these species are excellent to eat. They are pan-friend whole or as fillets.

SURFPERCHES
Family Embiotocidae

Life History
The surfperches are almost exclusively a Pacific Coast family. Two species occur in Japan, the other species are found primarily in the nearshore and estuarine habitats along the North American coast. One species, the tuleperch, *Hysterocarpus traski*, occurs only in fresh water.

The family name Embiotocidae means "living and bringing forth." The famous naturalist Louis Agassiz was the first to report that the surfperches gave birth to live young. This viviparous habit is rare among bony marine fishes. Most surfperches breed during the summer and fall when males deposit sperm with their modified anal fin into the female. The young develop, with most nutrition derived from the ovarian fluid. The young of most species appear during the spring and summer. Females generally produce 4 to 112 young (1 to 2 inches long) which look very much like the adults. The number and size of young varies by species but increases with age. In some species the males are sexually mature soon after birth. In general, both sexes are mature after 1 year. Some species live up to 10 years.

Surfperches occur in most coastal habits. True to their name, many species occur in the surf zone, which is rich in food. Typical of this group are the redtail (*Amphistichus rhodoterus*), barred (*Amphistichus argenteus*), and calico (*Amphistichus keolzi*) surfperches which occur along sandy beaches, where they feed primarily on sand crabs. Other species, such as the striped (*Embiotoca lateralis*) and rainbow (*Hypsurus caryi*) seaperches, prefer rocky bottoms. Several very abundant species frequent a wide variety of habitats: bays, river mouths, tidepools, kelp beds, and eel grass beds. The small shiner perch (*Cymatogaster aggregata*) and the black perch (*Embiotoca jacksoni*) are examples of the family members that occur in a wide variety of habitats.

Studies have shown surfperches to be omnivores and carnivores. Common food items include crabs, amphipods, worms, octopuses, limpets, snails, mussels, clams, and algae. Several species feed on parasites they remove from other nearshore fishes. The surfperches, especially the smaller ones, are important prey for large fish, birds, and marine mammals.

Fishery Information

Surfperch are landed by both commercial and recreational fishermen. The commercial landings are relatively small, usually less than 200,000 lb per year. Fishermen use beach seines and hook and line to land most of the catch. Surfperch are usually landed by part-time fishermen or by fishermen who also seek many other inshore fishes. The primary commercial species are the redtail, black, and white, *Phanerodon furcatus*, surfperches. There is also a small fishery for shiner perch for use as live bait.

Surfperch are an extremely important sportfish. Hundreds of thousands of anglers land surfperch from piers, beaches, and rocky shorelines. The abundant small shiner or walleye, *Hyperprosopon argenteum*, surfperch are the joyful first catch of many youthful anglers. The wily and large redtail, barred, calico, pile, (*Rhacochilus vacca*), and rubberlip,(*R. toxotes*),surfperches are often a challenge for the experienced angler. These fish grow commonly to 2 or 3 lb.

Baited hooks are the primary capture method. Mussels, pile worms, shrimps, crabs, and clams are favorite baits. Small lures and tiny feathered hooks sometimes work well. Anglers should remember that surfperch occur throughout the water column and shouldn't restrict their fishing to the bottom.

Consumer Information

Surfperch flesh has a delicate texture and sweet flavor. The smaller species are often gutted, scaled, and pan-fried whole. The larger species can be filleted. We often enjoy using these fish in fish chowders. Small quantities of whole surfperches are available to consumers all year in some seafood markets. They are most abundant in the spring and summer months all along the Pacific Coast.

BARRACUDAS
Family Sphyraenidae

Life History

The Pacific barracuda, *Sphyraena argentea*, is rare north of Morro Bay, California. These fish have long, slender, silvery bodies that enable them to capture prey with quick bursts of speed. They feed voraciously on anchovies, squid, and other small fishes.

Females are distinguished from males by black coloration on the anal and pelvic fins. Barracuda begin spawning when they are 2 or 3 years old, releasing approximately 40,000 pelagic eggs. Older fish may produce 500,000 eggs. They move northward from the population's center off Baja California during the spring and early summer and appear in the southern California's fishery at that time. Water temperatures seem to be important in determining the distribution and abundance of barracuda. Immature barracuda are often found in bays and harbors.

Fishery Information

The catches of barracuda have been declining steadily since they peaked at 8,000,000 lb in the 1920s. Decline in abundance, habitat degradation, fishing gear restrictions, and an erratic market demand have contributed to this decline in catches.

Most catches occur off southern California and northern Baja California. The commercial fishery began in the early 1900s and by the 1920s purse seiners were catching 6-8,000,000 lb annually. In more recent years barracuda have been taken primarily in gillnets and by hook and line.

Barracuda have been a mainstay of the southern California sportfishery until recent years. In many years anglers landed over 750,000 of the "scooters." Lures, live anchovies, and feathered jigs are the best baits. Wire leader is recommended because their sharp teeth will often cut through monofilament line.

Declining populations have concerned all those interested in the barracuda. In recent years a 28-inch size limit has been enforced to allow the fish to spawn once or twice before capture. Because of the transboundary nature of the stocks, any successful management depends on cooperation between California and Mexican fishery agencies.

Consumer Information

Various writers rate barracuda flesh between fair and excellent eating quality. If the fish are not gutted and chilled soon after capture, they tend to become soft. Like other fish, they are of highest quality if they are bled and gutted as soon as possible. Barracuda is delicious barbecued or smoked. The roe is also good.

Barracuda is marketed primarily in southern California. It appears whole, filleted, or smoked and is most available during the summer and fall months.

WRASSES
Family Labridae

Life History

Only three species of this striking and primarily tropical family are found along the Pacific Coast: the California sheephead (*Semicossyphus pulcher*), rock wrasses (*Halichoeres semicinctus*), and the senorita (*Oxyjulis californica*). All three species are associated with the inshore kelp bed areas of southern California.

Changing sexes like many wrasses, the sheephead spend the first 4 to 8 years as a rose-colored female. Then they change into males. As males, they change drastically in appearance by developing a blackish head and tail with a wide, bright pink bar across the middle of their body. During the breeding season, males grow a large bump on the top of their head. The sheephead uses its large, canine-like teeth to pry abalone, mussels, crabs, and sea urchins from rocks. They are apparently also fond of lobsters. The sheephead grows to at least 30 lb and can live for over 50 years.

The rock wrasse is another hermaphrodite like the sheephead. The male tends to be greenish-brown and has a dark blue band under the pectoral fins. The female is orange-brown with small black spots. Rock wrasses feed during the day on small crustaceans and molluscs, and then hide under rocks at night. They spawn during the summer. Their maximum size is 15 inches.

Fishery Information

These fish are primarily an incidental catch for recreational anglers. A small commercial fishery exists for sheephead, but the landings never exceed a few thousand pounds annually. Crab, abalone trimmings, mussels, and shrimp are good baits for the sheephead. Rock wrasses are easily captured with most baits on small hooks. They are not highly prized.

Consumer Information

Many people falsely believe that sheephead are not a good food fish. It is quite similar to rockfish in texture and can be prepared in similar ways. Some people use sheephead for chowder. Sheephead are rarely seen in markets.

WOLFFISHES
Family Anarhichadidae

Life History

The wolf-eel, *Anarrhichthys ocellatus*, is not a true eel. This eel-like fish is common from Point Conception, California, to the Aleutian Islands. They are large and fearsome in appearance. Wolf-eels grow to be 6.5 ft and 40 lb. They inhabit rock reef areas, often near sandy areas. They feed primarily on invertebrates, crabs being their favorite fare.

Recent studies have shown that wolf-eels are quite territorial. They reside in rocky areas during the day and roam over large areas at night in search of food. The next morning they return to their original rocky home. They spawn during the winter and both parents guard the nest. Young wolf-eels usually have beautiful yellow spots on their bodies. These spots disappear as they mature.

Fishery Information

Anglers and spearfishermen capture wolf-eels in small numbers. The best baits are abalone, mussels, crabs, and anchovies. Care should be taken in handling captured wolf-eels because of their sharp teeth and strong jaws. Wolf-eels are edible.

MACKERELS
Family Scombridae

Life History

Tunas and mackerels are primarily pelagic fish; they range widely throughout the world's surface waters. Many species migrate thousands of miles and their distribution is strongly related to oceanographic conditions that influence the production and concentration of prey.

Tunas and mackerels must swim at all times to insure an adequate flow of oxygen across their gills. Scombrids use their speed and sharp senses to locate large amounts of food. Unlike most fish, tuna maintain a body temperature above that of the water. This elevated temperature apparently enables the fish to respond quickly and to digest food quickly.

Members of this family have evolved many features that increase their speed and protect them from predation. Their bodies are streamlined and smooth. The tunas' fins fit down into grooves which reduce water resistance. Their moon-shaped tail provides excellent forward thrust. The tunas provide a good example of countershading in fishes. They are dark on top, which makes them nearly invisible to birds and other predators above but are silvery and white below, which makes it difficult for upward-looking predators to separate them from the light glare of surface waters.

Tunas and mackerels lay large numbers of tiny (0.04-inch) eggs. Females lay approximately 50,000 eggs per pound of body weight. The few young that survive the first months of life grow rapidly. Yellowfin tuna reach 6 lb in their first year and grow to over 100 lb by their 4th year. They feed on fish, squid, and crustaceans. Some species will eat up to 25% of their weight per day. The largest members of this family are the yellowfin and the bluefin tunas, which reach a maximum size of over 350 and 1,500 lb, respectively.

Tunas are usually associated with tropical waters, but several species occur in the more temperate water found along the Pacific Coast. These species include Pacific or chub mackerel (*Scomber japonicus*), Pacific bonito (*Sarda chiliensis*), and albacore (*Thunnus alalunga*). Several other species are captured in large numbers throughout the tropical Pacific and landed primarily in southern California. These include yellowfin tuna (*Thunnus albacares*), skipjack (*Euthynnus pelamis*), bigeye tuna (*Thunnus obesus*), and bluefin tuna (*Thunnus thynnus*).

Fishery Information

Members of this family are extremely valuable commercial and recreational fish. The world catch in 1978 was over 2.5 million metric tons worth at least $1.5 billion. Tuna are caught by pole and line, purse seine, trolling gear, and longline.

Annually, hundreds of millions of pounds of tuna (primarily yellowfin and skipjack), which are caught throughout the world, are landed in San Diego and San Pedro. These tuna are caught primarily purse seines and by pole and line, frozen on board the large, modern vessels, and delivered back to California canneries. Although this has been a lucrative fishery in the past, the industry now faces many serious problems. These include other nations' claims of management jurisdiction of tuna in their coastal waters out to 200 miles, rising fuel costs, marketing problems, overcapitalization and potential overharvesting, lack of cooperation between tuna fish nations, and fishing restrictions to protect marine mammals. The future of the fishery appears to depend more on the industry's ability to negotiate with other nations rather than fishing ability.

Albacore tuna are landed in California, Oregon, and Washington. The fishery began off southern California in the early 1900s and it became a coast-wide fishery in the mid-1930s. Landings have varied widely between 5,000,000 and 65,000,000 lb annually. Over the last 20 years, the landings have averaged about 40,000,000 lb per year. The last 4 years have been very poor and there is some concern that expanded Japanese fishing efforts in the central Pacific are reducing the number of fish available to American fishermen.

Albacore make long migrations. There apparently are at least two substocks. The northern (above 40° N) group migrates all the way across the Pacific. The southern stock appear to migrate less and grow more rapidly. Fishermen try to intercept the albacore on their migrations. Generally albacore appear off our shores in the summer or fall. They tend to favor waters between 50° and 68°F. Fishermen search for albacore in areas where sharp differences in water temperatures concentrate baitfish. In recent years, fishermen have begun to work further offshore (1,500 to 2,000 miles) to intercept fish earlier.

Unlike many other tunas and mackerels, albacore travel in loose schools. Therefore, purse seines are generally ineffective. Most albacore are landed by 50- to 90-ft vessels that troll feathered jigs or use live bait. The trollers travel at 5 to 8 knots and search widely for schools of fish. The bait boats will often troll to locate fish concentrations and then they use live anchovies to attract the school for pole and line fishing. Recently, an experimental winter tuna fishery using longline 800-900 miles west of San Diego has shown promise for expanding the season. The longlines are fished at or above the thermocline, the area of sharp temperature difference between sun-warmed surface waters and colder deep waters, usually located at a depth of over 300 ft.

The recreational fishery for albacore is also important. Most sportfishing vessels troll to locate schools and then use live bait for fishing. Because the sportfishermen generally have less range than the commercial fishermen, catches depend on how close albacore come to shore. Annual party boat landings of albacore have varied from near zero to over 200,000 fish per year.

The Pacific mackerel historically has been one of California's leaders in tonnage landed. During the 1930s and 1940s landings often exceeded 100,000,000 lb. By the 1960s the catch had dwindled to near zero and protective regulations were implemented. The decline apparently was due to heavy fishing and to several very weak year classes. Their schooling behavior makes mackerel vulnerable to over-harvesting. Today, the Pacific mackerel resource appears to be making a come-back and landings are rising in both the recreational and commercial fisheries.

Consumer Information

Almost all tuna and mackerel is canned. About 75% of the world tuna catch is consumed in the United States and Japan. What seems like an everyday food to us is an expensive luxury for the rest of the world.

One reason for canning tuna is that most of it is landed in a whole, frozen form. This frozen state, plus the large size of most tunas, makes them difficult for the retailer and consumer to handle. Albacore is usually marketed as "white-meated tuna," while yellowfin and skip-jack are generally "light-meated tuna."

In 1982, large amounts of albacore were marketed directly by fishermen because of extremely low cannery prices. It appears that there is a market for fresh or frozen tuna. They are delicious raw ("sashimi"), barbecued, fried, broiled, or home-canned.

Most albacore tuna are marketed frozen during the summer and fall months. Whole albacore can be ordered through most seafood markets during those months. After cutting the loins off of the fish, it can be cooked, home-canned, or refrozen for later use. Other tunas are landed year-round and fresh tuna is often available through Oriental seafood markets.

Recreational fishermen who catch mackerel or tuna should bleed them immediately by cutting the gills and/or tail. This will improve the color, keeping quality, and flavor of the fish. The fish should be gutted promptly and kept cool.

The tunas are high in both oil and protein. Albacore contain approximately 10% oil and 25% protein.

FLATFISHES
Families Bothidae and Pleuronectidae

Life History

The flatfishes—flounders, soles, and halibut—make up one of most important groups of Pacific Coast demersal fishes. When flatfish eggs hatch into pelagic larvae, they have eyes on each side of the head like other fishes. After a while, one eye migrates over the top of the head. Once both eyes are on one side of the flatfish's head, the flatfish settles down to the bottom with its "two-eyed" side up.

The two major Pacific Coast flatfish families are the left-eyed flounders (Bothidae) and the right-eyed flounders (Pleuronectidae). The most reliable way to tell the two families apart is to hold the fish dorsal side up with the head facing away from you. If the eyes are on the left side of the head, it is left-eyed (Bothidae); all others are in the family Pleuronectidae. Some pleuronectids, such as the starry flounder, often have eyes on the left side of the head rather than on the right side.

Halibut are the most famous of the flatfishes. Two species are common: the California halibut, *Paralichthys californicus*, and the Pacific halibut, *Hippoglossus stenolepis*. These species are quite different. California halibut belong to the family Bothidae and are most common in central and southern California. They occur primarily in shallow waters (less than 150 ft deep). They prey on croakers, anchovies, and octopuses over sandy bottoms. They migrate into shallow water of less than 60 ft to spawn during the spring. California halibut grow to over 60 lb and live at least 30 years. The females tend to grow faster and larger than the males.

The Pacific halibut belongs to the family Pleuronectidae and is common north of Washington. The Pacific halibut lays several million eggs in deep water. The young fish settle to the bottom at about 5 inches and feed heavily on fish and shellfish with their large, tooth-filled mouths. Males generally are less than 100 lb, while females grow to well over 500 lb.

Two other flatfishes are especially important and unique. The starry flounder, *Platichthys stellatus*, is the only flatfish that occurs in large bays, sloughs, and even well up some coastal rivers. They feed primarily on small crustaceans, clams, and worms. The Dover sole, *Microstomus pacificus*, is one of the most common deep water fishes. Along with the sablefish, the Dover sole is often the most abundant fish on the continental shelf as deep as 4,000 ft. They make annual migrations in the fall to these depths for winter spawning. After spawning, the Dover sole moves back into shallower areas, 600 to 1,200 ft deep, where they feed on invertebrates associated with muddy bottoms. The Dover sole is a slow grower; it takes 8 years for them to reach 16 inches in length.

Fishery Information

The flatfishes are extremely valuable. Except for the two halibut, most flatfish are captured in otter trawls dragged across the bottom.

The large Pacific halibut was captured with hook and line by coastal Indians long before European settlers came. By the early 1900s a substantial longline fishery had developed. The commercial fishery has been centered in Alaska where the resource is most abundant. Landings have ranged from 44 to 75,000,000 lb annually. Because of the halibut's great value, many fishermen have been attracted into the fishery. To protect the fishery, the International Pacific Halibut Commission (IPHC) has set seasons, gear restrictions, and quotas. In some areas the quota is taken within a week or two of intense fishing. In 1982, the controversial concept of having fishermen bid for individual quotas began to receive consideration. Another concern is the incidental take of young halibut by foreign trawlers fishing in Alaskan waters.

The California halibut fishery is conducted primarily in shallow water with trammel and gillnets. The catch has been as high as 3,500,000 lb (1917), but has stabilized at 1 to 2,000,000 lb in recent years. California halibut are a prized sportfish also, with landings exceeding 100,000 fish in some years. Live bait drifted along the bottom is the primary method used.

Numerous smaller flatfishes are captured in trawls and support an important part of the fishing industry. The primary species in the trawl fishery are: Dover sole, English sole (*Parophrys vetulus*), petrale sole (*Eopsetta jordani*), rex sole (*Glyptocephalus zachirus*), sanddabs (*Citharichthys sordidus* and *C. stigmaeus*), sand sole (*Psettichthys melanostictus*), and starry flounder. These flatfish often occur at slightly different depths over different bottom types and fishermen will sometimes target on one species (e.g. sanddabs, Dover sole). The Pacific Coast trawl fleet in California, Oregon, and Washington landed about 30,000,000 lb of flatfish in 1982.

Consumer Information

The flatfish tend to be lean (less than 2 gm fat per 100 gm) and low in calories (85 calories per 100 gm). Most of the flatfish have a very delicate flavor and texture.

The larger number of flatfish species and confusing names make it difficult for the consumer to know which species he is eating. Fillet of sole usually comes from Dover, petrale, English, or sand sole. Each species has different textures and flavors, with the Dover sole tending to be softer than most. Rex sole and sanddabs are marketed headed and gutted in a whole form. These species are usually pan-fried or sauteed. Flounders and California halibut are generally filleted, while the large Pacific halibut is cut into steaks.

Trawl-caught flatfish such as Dover sole, English sole, and petrale sole are available in filleted form all year. Smaller flatfish such as sanddabs and rex sole are sold year-round. The two halibut species are much more seasonal. The large Pacific halibut is caught primarily in May and June and marketed primarily as frozen and thawed steaks throughout the year. The smaller California halibut is most common in markets during the spring and summer as fresh fillets.

ABALONE
Family Haliotidae

Life History

Abalone are found along the entire Pacific Coast, with the greatest species diversity and populations in California. These large, snail-like organisms of the genus *Haliotis* live in shallow waters; they are most common in waters less than 100 ft deep. Most of the eight common species prefer wave-battered rocky coasts with good stands of kelp.

In general, abalone spawning appears to be triggered by warming water temperatures. The male releases sperm, which induces the female to release large numbers of tiny eggs. The fertilized eggs go through approximately 11 planktonic larval stages within 10 days. They feed on tiny plankton (diatoms and flagellates). The surviving larvae settle on algae-encrusted areas, where they feed on attached diatoms. After 6 months or so the abalone begin to feed on algae such as kelp, which will remain their primary food for the rest of their life. Although growth rates vary considerably between species and locations, abalone grow about 1 inch per year for their first 8 years. After that time their growth slows. The red abalone, *Haliotis rufescens*, the world's largest abalone, grows to 12 inches.

In addition to man, abalone have several predators. The cabezon, moray eel, sheephead, rock crab, octopus, and sun star feed on abalone. The sea otter is also a voracious predator of abalone.

Fishery Information

Abalone are prized as food throughout the world. The United States, Australia, Mexico, South Africa, and Korea have major fisheries. The Pacific Coast fishery has been centered in California, although small fisheries for the pinto abalone, *Haliotis kamtschatkana*, have developed in recent years in Washington and southeastern Alaska. California fishermen harvest primarily five species; red abalone is the largest and most valuable species.

Historically, Indians harvested abalone for food; they used the shells for jewelry. In the 1800s the Chinese immigrants developed the California commercial fishery in intertidal areas with landings as high as 4,000,000 lb. By 1900 laws banning the commercial take of abalone in waters less than 20 ft eliminated the non-diving Chinese from the fishery. Japanese divers became the primary harvesters in the first half of this century. Since the 1950s, with the development of efficient diving gear, Caucasian fishermen have entered the fishery in large numbers.

During the past 50 years, the commercial fishery has shifted southward from Monterey to Santa Barbara, where the more common pink abalone, *Haliotis corrugata*, is the primary target species. Catches in the 1950s approached 6,000,000 lb, but have recently declined to less than 1,000,000 lb annually.

Three reasons are cited for the decline: overfishing, pollution, and increased predation by sea otters. New regulations limiting the number of fishermen, raising size limits, and experimentally closing some fishing areas are designed to maintain the resource and the economic viability of the fishery. Experimental seeding programs, artificial reefs, and kelp restoration projects are now used to try to mitigate for the impacts of pollution.

Sea otter predation is a major issue in the fishery. Since the early 1900s sea otters have been completely protected in California. Russian hunters decimated the otter population in the mid-1800s. Under protection, the sea otter population has grown from only 50 to 1,200 animals (approximately 120,000 sea otters live in Alaska) and the range has expanded to include the coast between Pismo Beach and Santa Cruz. The sea otter is on the Federal Threatened Species list primarily because of the danger that a major oil spill would jeopardize the entire population.

Man's fishery for abalone grew during a time when abalone populations increased due to the absence of the sea otter. In areas where sea otters have re-established populations, viable abalone fisheries no longer exist. The major issue is whether sea otter populations should be limited to allow for viable shellfish fisheries. Shellfish fishermen generally say "yes," but many others disagree. State and federal agencies, fishermen, and citizen groups are beginning to work together to resolve this issue. Proposals include translocation of otters to other locations, zonal management with some areas for shellfish fisheries and others for otters, and increased emphasis on abalone culture to enhance or replace the wild fishery.

The high price and world demand make abalone an attractive aquaculture animal. Landings from the wild fishery cannot satisfy the world demand. Over half the abalone consumed in California is imported from Mexico, while Japan imports tens of millions of dollars worth of abalone annually. Rearing of abalone (aquaculture) is being pursued intensely in California. Abalone are reared in tanks on shore and in offshore artificial habitats. Due to their slow growth rate, most abalone are grown to sizes of less than 3 inches and sold live to restaurants or to groups involved in reseeding programs. The major constraints to the abalone aquaculture industry are the high cost of coastal land, slow growth of abalone, problems with artificial habitat design, and high mortality rates at some post-larval stages.

Recreational anglers take significant numbers of abalone. The method of harvest depends on state regulations. Anglers pry abalone off rocks during low tides with an abalone iron, free dive for them in shallow waters, or use scuba gear in southern California.

Consumer Information

Most abalone is sold to restaurants or consumers as tenderized steaks. These steaks are usually breaded and then fried for less than 1 minute on each side. Due to high cost and inconsistent supply, abalone is not common in seafood stores. Abalone waste products are valuable. The trimmed edges are ground and used as patties and the shells are sold to tourists.

If you capture your own abalone, they can be prepared in several ways. When you get home, remove the abalone from the shell. Trim off the black edges, cut in ¼-inch thick steaks, and then pound until tender. Save the trimmings and guts in jars with rock salt because they are excellent bait. Abalone is also good sliced paper-thin and eaten raw with teriyaki sauce. Others recipes use whole, boiled abalone.

Abalone is relatively low in protein (15 gm per 100 gm) and extremely low in fat (0.5 gm per 100 gm).

SCALLOPS
Family Pectinidae

Life History

Scallops are bivalve (two-shelled) mollusks closely related to clams, oysters, and mussels. Scallops are unique in this group because they are capable of moving through the water for part or all of their lives. They propel themselves by rapidly closing their shells and forcing water out between holes near their hinge.

Scallops release millions of sperm and eggs, and the larvae settle to the bottom after 4 to 6 weeks. Like other bivalves, scallops strain food out of the large quantities of water pumped over their gills. Scallops grow to 10 to 12 inches wide and live at least 20 years. The rock scallop, *Hinnities multirugosus*, is unique among Pacific scallops because it cements itself to a rock at 6 months of age and remains there

for life. The spawning success, especially of the weathervane scallop, *Patinopecten caurinus*, appears to vary greatly from year to year due to changing oceanographic conditions.

Fishery Information

The rock scallop is harvested by recreational divers and commercial abalone pickers in tidepools and nearshore rocky areas. Rock scallops are often found on breakwaters and pilings. Recently University of California Sea Grant researchers have developed culture techniques for growing rock scallops. There appears to be some acquaculture potential, and some oyster growers have started to rear a few scallops.

The weathervane scallop has been sporadically fished in Alaska, with high catches in some years. In 1981 two New Jersey scallop vessels heading for the Alaskan fishery discovered a scallop bed off Oregon. Within a few months over 100 vessels were fishing there for scallops. Close to 10,000,000 lb were harvested (1,000,000 lb of meats). Gear and processing costs, and marketing problems kept profits low. The fishery was based almost entirely on one successful year class (7-year-olds). By the end of 1981 the scallop beds were fished down to such low levels that only a few boats could profitably fish. It appears that spawning success is sporadic and that the fishery will be a small one except during years when very successful year classes of scallops reach commercial size.

Commercial scallop fishing is done primarily with dredges which are made up of connected steel rings that form a small, heavy net. The dredge is dragged right on the bottom. Small otter trawls are also used, but they are not as efficient and they tend to catch more small fishes than the dredges.

Consumer Information

The large, white muscle is the part commonly eaten. The viscera are usually discarded. Like many other filter-feeding bivalves, scallops can cause paralytic shellfish poisoning. In 1981 a diver died after eating raw viscera of a rock scallop.

The scallop is usually fried, sauteed, or baked. It has excellent flavor and is low in fat (0.7 gm per 100 gm). Most scallops sold on the Pacific Coast are from the Atlantic Ocean. These frozen Atlantic scallops are available throughout the year. The smaller variety are known as bay scallops. In recent years some scallops captured off Oregon and Alaska have sporadically appeared in markets.

OYSTERS
Family Ostreidae

Life History

Of the four important Pacific Coast oysters only one is native. The native Olympia oyster, *Ostrea lurida*, is the smallest of the four species. The three exotic species were introduced by companies interested in improving oyster aquaculture along the Pacific Coast.

Oysters are bivalves closely related to clams and mussels. The mature adults may change their sex several times during their life. Females release 25,000 (Olympia oyster) to 60,000,000 eggs (Pacific oyster). The free-swimming larvae drift and feed for about 3 weeks before seeking a hard surface to settle on. When the larva finds a rock or shell (cultch), it secretes a bit of cement from its byssus gland and attaches itself for life. The native oyster is the smallest, taking perhaps 5 years to reach 2 inches. The Pacific oyster, *Crassostrea gigas*, is the largest, growing to 6 or 7 inches within 2 to 3 years.

Fishery Information

Until the 1850s the native Olympia oyster was the only oyster harvested. Increased demand and pollution during the 1850s led to the devastation of the native oyster resources along the coast. The larger, faster-growing eastern oyster, *Crassostrea virginica*, was transplanted into San Francisco and other bays. Two to 3,000,000 lb of meat were produced annually. In 1904 oysters were the most valuable fishery in California. Jack London wrote stories about oyster pirates and their lucrative business.

By the 1920s pollution and habitat degradation had depressed the industry. Pacific Coast production fell to 750,000 lb. In the 1930s the Pacific oyster, *Crassostrea gigas*, was introduced from Japan. This oyster grew faster and larger than the eastern oyster and was quickly adopted by the industry. Due to continued pollution problems in San Francisco Bay, the oyster industry shifted primarily to Washington. Today, at least 80% of the Pacific Coast oyster production comes from Washington. The fourth important species, the European oyster, *Ostrea edulis*, was imported to rear experimentally in modern aquaculture operations. This oyster is highly esteemed in Europe.

The great majority of oysters are reared rather than harvested from the wild. Historically, Olympia oysters were collected in the wild. Today there is a small recreational fishery for Olympia and Pacific oysters in the Puget Sound and British Columbia areas.

None of the exotic oysters reproduce consistently in Pacific waters. The water temperatures are too cold (below 65°F). At a few locations in Washington and British Columbia, Pacific oysters reproduce well enough to supply part of the seed for the industry. Often oyster growers must rely on imported seed oysters for their operations. Several companies are attempting to develop oyster hatcheries to reproduce seed for the industry.

Oysters are grown in bays with good current flow and plankton populations. Seed oysters, usually attached to cultch, are spread over leased grow-out areas or they are suspended on ropes from rafts or poles. The oysters grown suspended above the bottom grow about twice as fast, but it is a more expensive technique. After 1 to 3 years, the oysters are harvested.

Consumer Information

Pacific oysters are sold primarily in the shell or shucked in small jars. Besides being high in protein and low in fat, they contain numerous important trace minerals. Oysters are rumored to be good for your sex life, although some have found sea urchin roe to be superior.

Oysters are eaten raw, steamed, fried, baked, and used in soups. They are often graded by size with the smaller sizes prepared for the half-shell trade. Oysters on the half-shell with hot sauce, lemon, or horseradish are a treat.

CLAMS   and   MUSSELS
Class Bivalvia   Family Mytilidae

Life History

A great variety of clams, 160 species in Alaska alone, occur along the Pacific Coast. Several important species are not native, but were introduced accidentally with oyster shipments or by ships. They live in a wide variety of habitats including sandy beaches, muddy bay bottoms, rocks, and muddy offshore bottoms. Instead of generalizing about their life history, I'll discuss a few important species.

Two species, the Pismo clam and the razor clam, are extremely important along ocean beaches. The Pismo clam, *Tivela stultorum*, is common south of central California. They begin spawning during the summer of their second year. They release about 15,000,000 eggs. The larvae are free-swimming for at least several weeks before settling into the sand. They grow ½ to ¼ of an inch during each of their first 5 years and live up to 35 years (weight of 4 lb). They siphon out planktonic organisms and detritus from 15 or more gallons of water per day. The razor clam, *Siliqua patula*, is common from northern California through Alaska. They mature at 18 months and release 6 to 10,000,000 eggs which are fertilized externally. The larvae are free-swimming for 5 to 16 weeks before currents deliver them to the beach, where they settle out. They feed on plankton and grow to 4½ inches with 2 years.

The butter or smooth Washington clam, *Saxidomus giganteus*, is very common north of Humboldt Bay, California. It is typical of the type of hardshell clams found in mud and sandy mud bottoms of estuaries. The butter clam lives at depths of 10 to 14 inches in intertidal and subtidal areas. Other clams commonly found in estuarine habitats are the gaper (*Schizothaerus nuttalli*), cockles (*Clinocardian* sp.), Washington clam (*Saxidomus nuttalli*), littlenecks (*Protothaca staminea* and *Tapes semidecussata*), soft-shell clam (*Mya arenaria*), and the huge geoduck (*Panope generosa*).

The two most common mussels along the Pacific Coast are the California sea mussel, *Mytilus californianus*, and the bay or blue mussel, *Mytilus edulis*. The sea mussel is more common along surf-battered, rocky ocean shores, while the bay mussel is found in quieter waters. Mussels, like clams, have numerous pelagic larvae that drift with the currents. When they settle out, they attach themselves to rocks, pilings, and other solid objects with thin, strong threads.

Fishery Information

Large commercial and recreational fisheries occur along the Pacific Coast. Washington, British Columbia, and Alaska have much more clam habitat than either Oregon or California. The commercial fishery has operated primarily in Washington and Alaska, where huge clam resources are largely untouched.

Recreational clammers are most successful during extreme (minus) low tides. They walk along beaches or mudflats looking for characteristic siphon holes of some clams and just dig or use a rake to bring them up. Capturing razor clams is the most challenging. Clammers walk along sandy ocean beaches pounding sand with the end of a shovel handle. When a disturbed razor clam retracts its siphon, the clammer places the shovel about 6 inches seaward of the clam. By pulling on the handle, the sand is compacted and the fast-digging razor clam is usually prevented from pulling itself out of reach. The clammer then reaches down and finds the clam before a wave fills his boots with icy water. A different challenge is offered by the largest Pacific burrowing clam, the geoduck. Geoducks live at depths of 4 or more feet in the sand-mud bottoms of bays. The clammer must try to dig a deep hole that doesn't collapse before the clam is reached.

The Pacific commercial clam fishery has historically been centered in Washington because of the relatively large resource. The razor clam fishery used to be significant, but now most of that resource is allocated to recreational clammers. There is a small commercial fishery operated by the Quinault Indians, who harvest about 250,000 lb per year. The bulk of Washington clam fishing is based on several species of hard shell clams: littlenecks, Manilas, butters, and geoducks. In 1975 the leading species were the manila (963,745 lb) and the geoduck (2,400,000 lb).

Several methods are used to harvest the clams commercially. Dredges are the primary method used for littlenecks and butter clams. Manila clams, *Venerupis japonica*, are harvested by hand because they live so close to the surface. The large geoduck fishery, which developed in the 1970s, is limited to divers using suction devices to extract these large animals. State bottoms are leased by auction to geoduck harvesters.

The Alaskan clam resource is huge. The potential surf clam maximum sustainable yield has been estimated at approximately 60,000,000 lb. Other clams such as razor clams, butter clams, cockles, and soft-shell clams could produce many millions of pounds annually. The main restrictions in developing the Alaskan fishery are the expense of transportation, concern about paralytic shellfish poisoning, high labor costs, and a shortage of harvesters.

A significant recreational fishery for mussels exists along rocky shores. Many ethnic groups prize mussels as food. Mussels are also take for bait. A small aquaculture industry is developing to meet the increasing demand for bay mussels in restaurants and seafood markets. Much of the culture technology has been highly developed in other nations, such as Spain and Chile.

Consumer Information

Clams and mussels are prepared in numerous ways. The larger, tougher clams such as the gaper and butter clams are usually chopped up and used in chowder. Smaller clams are either eaten raw or steamed. Razor clams are fried. Mussels are usually steamed.

Commercially harvested clams and mussels are closely monitored by health departments for paralytic shellfish poisoning and bacterial contamination. Recreational clam and mussel harvesters should be aware of any local restrictions on harvesting or consumption. If in doubt, check with your local Department of Health. Many harvesting areas have warnings posted and mussels are often quarantined from late spring through late fall.

Clams and mussels are available all year in markets. Except in Washington, most of the clams and shellfish are shipped live from the Atlantic Coast. Many markets have installed salt water tanks to hold these shellfish, so they may be sold live. Clams and mussels in good condition will live for several days, if kept cool.

MARKET SQUID
Family Lolinginidae

Life History

Although a number of squid species occur along the Pacific Coast, the market squid, *Loligo opalescens*, is the most thoroughly studied and exploited.

The market squid is the most common squid in nearshore waters between Baja California and British Columbia. Adult squid migrate into water less than 100 ft deep to spawn. Spawning begins during winter in southern California and occurs progressively later further north. A female extrudes 20 to 30 egg capsules, each containing 180 to 300 eggs. Squid die soon after spawning.

Larval squid hatch in about a month; however, little is known about them until they reach maturity. Market squid are relatively small, reaching a total length of 12 inches. Though most scientists report *Loligo opalescens* living 3 years, recent studies indicate that they may live only 18 months.

Squid feed on shrimp-like euphausiids, copepods, fish, and other squid. Squid are extremely important prey for sharks, fishes, seabirds, marine mammals, and man.

Fishery Information

Chinese fishermen began harvesting squid in Monterey Bay in 1863. They used torches to attract squid to the surface where they captured them with small purse seines. In 1905 the lampara net was introduced by Italian fishermen and the landings grew to 19,000 tons by the late 1940s. In Monterey squid are still captured by locating spawning aggregations and setting large lampara nets around the spawning squid.

In the 1950s a fishery developed off southern California using different methods. The squid are attracted to the vessel with bright lights at night and then scooped up with a large, sock-like dipnet called a brail. This southern fishery has grown in size to equal the Monterey fishery.

The market squid resource appears to be capable of supporting a much larger harvest during some years. The major constraint to the expansion is the lack of a large market demand. It is hoped that mechanized squid-cleaning machines will make squid products attractive to the American consumer. Fishermen in Oregon, Washington, and Alaska began exploring for market squid concentrations in 1981 and 1982. If consistent concentrations are found and processing facilities and markets are developed, the squid fishery could expand significantly.

In some years a large squid, *Dosidicus gigas*, is found off southern California. In the 1970s a substantial fishery developed off Mexico. This squid, which grows to 200 lb, is marketed in the United States as "grande calamari." Its flesh resembles abalone in appearance and texture.

Recreational anglers can capture squid to eat or for bait. Small, shiny lures or feathered hooks are effective. When the large *Dosidicus* appears, they are prized by fishermen.

Print 32   Striped Bass   *Morone saxatilis*

Print 33   Kelp Bass   *Paralabrax clathratus*

Print 34   Jack Mackerel   *Trachurus symmetricus*

Print 35   Yellowtail   *Seriola lalandei*

Print 36   Pacific Pomfret   *Brama japonica*

Print 37   White Croaker   *Genyonemus lineatus*

Print 38   Opaleye   *Girella nigricans*

Print 39   Halfmoon   *Medialuna californiensis*

Print 40 **Walleye Surfperch** *Hyperprosopon argenteum*

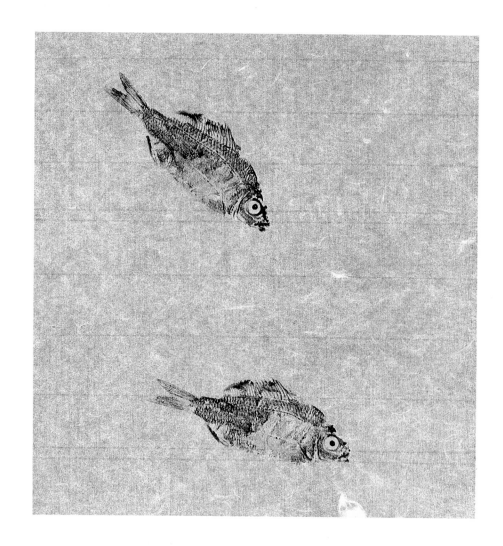

Print 41   Shiner Perch   *Cymatogaster aggregata*

Print 42   Striped Seaperch   *Embiotoca lateralis*

Print 43   Pile Perch   *Rhacochilus vacca*

Print 44   Pacific Barracuda   *Sphyraena argentea*

Print 45   California Sheephead   *Semicossyphus pulcher*

Print 46   Rock Wrasse *Halichoeres semicinctus*   male   female

Print 47   Wolf-Eel   *Anarrhichthys ocellatus*

Print 48   Chub Mackerel *Scomber japonicus*

Print 49   Albacore   *Thunnus alalunga*

Print 50 California Halibut *Paralichthys californicus*

Print 51   Rock Sole   *Lepidopsetta bilineata*

Print 52   Starry Flounder   *Platichthys stellatus*

Print 53　Petrale Sole　*Eopsetta jordani*

Print 54 Red Abalone *Haliotis rufescens*

Print 55   Rock Scallop   *Hinnites multirugosus*

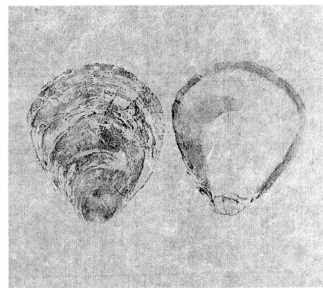

Print 56   Weathervane Scallop   *Patinopectin caurinus*
European Oyster   *Ostrea edulis*

Print 57   Geoduck Clam   *Panope generosa*

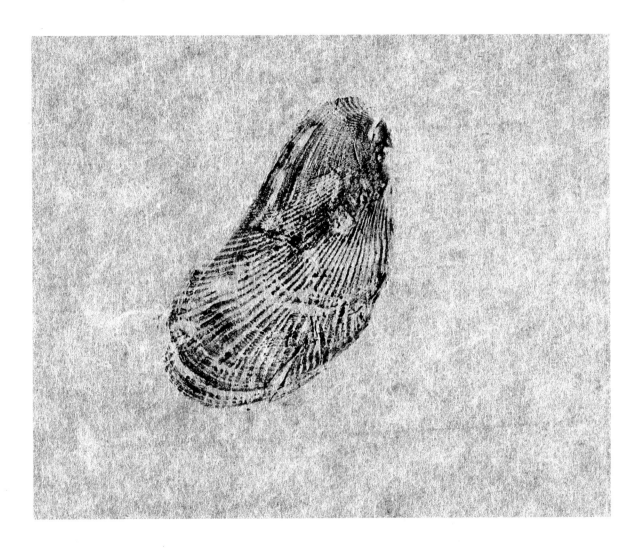

Print 58 Ribbed Horse Mussel *Ischadium demissum*

Print 59   Market Squid   *Loligo opalescens*

Print 60   Octopus   *Octopus* sp.

Print 61   Dungeness Crab   *Cancer magister*

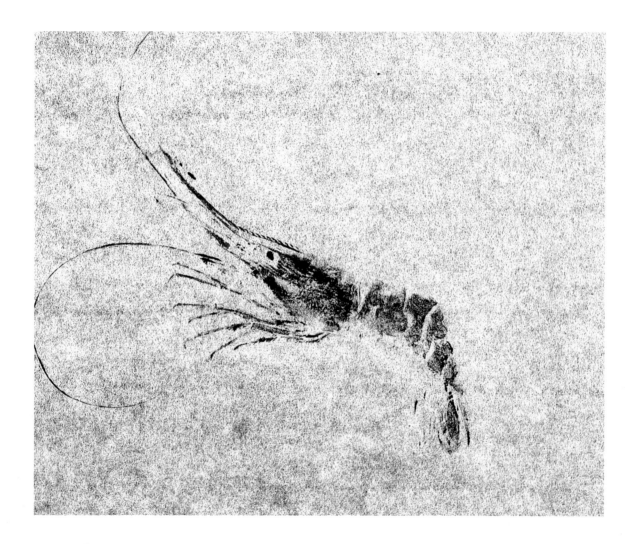

Print 62   Spot Prawn   *Pandalus platyceros*

Print 63   Southern Kelp Bed Fishes

Consumer Information

Squid is delicious, high in protein (15 gm per 100 gm), and low in fat (1 gm per 100 gm) and calories (89 calories per 100 gm). It is relatively inexpensive, often less than $1 per pound whole. Relatively few people enjoy squid because they don't know how to clean and prepare it.

Recently, Sea Grant researchers at U.C. Davis have developed a prototype squid-cleaning machine designed especially for *Loligo opalescens*. If this machine is successfully adapted to meet industry needs, low-cost, cleaned squid will be available to the consumer.

Squid is rarely marketed fresh because it is highly perishable. Most squid is frozen whole within a few hours after it is landed. Squid is available throughout the year frozen or thawed in most markets. Some squid is also canned, primarily for export. Occasionally squid speciality products such as rings, breaded cutlets, or stuffed squid are marketed. As more squid is cleaned mechanically, there will probably be an increased availability of speciality products.

OCTOPUSES
Family Octopodidae

Life History

Octopuses are the most intelligent of the invertebrates. They have large brains and large eyes and they seem to be capable of learning. Octopuses have eight sucker-covered arms, but they lack the two additional tentacles found in squid. Male octopuses are identified by the presence of a third right arm, which has a spade-shaped, suckerless tip that is used to transfer sperm packets into the female during reproduction.

Of the half dozen common species of Pacific Coast octopuses, the giant Pacific octopus, *Octopus dofleini*, is the largest and best known. The giant octopus is common from northern California northward to the Aleutian Islands and southward to Korea. This huge octopus can grow to a weight of 600 lb during its 4- to 5-year life span.

Breeding appears to take place most of the year, with a peak during the late fall. The eggs are guarded by the female. The young larval octopuses hatch and spend about a month actively swimming in the plankton before settling down to the bottom.

The giant octopus is a voracious predator that grows quickly. They feed on crabs, shrimps, clams, abalones, scallops, snails, and fishes. A sharp beak and toxin in the saliva help them conquer hard-to-penetrate shellfish. The giant octopus is preyed upon by marine mammals, large fishes, and man.

Fishery Information

Historically, the Japanese have been the world's most productive octopus fishermen. They use traps and longlines. A small fishery exists along the Pacific Coast, primarily in Washington's Puget Sound. In recent years, interest has grown in the octopus fishery because of potential markets in Alaska for octopus to be used as halibut bait and among certain ethnic groups in large urban centers.

Much of the catch is taken incidentally by bottom trawlers fishing for other species. It is likely that these catches increase during periods when the octopuses are making migrations to and from deep waters. Smaller octopuses (less than 25 lb) are preferred by buyers.

A small octopus fishery using traps exists. The traps are constructed of any material that provides shelter for the octopus and is stable on the bottom. The unbaited traps, usually wooden boxes, are set on sandy or muddy areas with plenty of prey for octopus. The octopuses feed at night and hide in a lair during the day. The traps work because they provide daytime shelter for the octopus. The traps are inexpensive to build and only need to be checked once or twice per week.

The octopus resource, particulary in Alaska, appears to be large. With improved markets and declines in other fisheries, we are likely to see a modest increase in octopus landings. The fast growth rate of octopuses has also attracted the interest of aquaculturists.

Consumer Information

Octopuses are available most of the year at many seafood markets. The larger octopuses seen in markets from northern California to Alaska are usually the giant Pacific octopus. Small octopuses are primarily imported from Spain, African, Japan, or Mexico. If a market doesn't have octopus, they can usually order it for you.

Because octopus is usually tough, it needs to be tenderized by pounding, pressure cooking, or slicing the cooked meat into very thin pieces. Another method involves pressure cooking the octopus for

45 minutes, removing the skin and shredding the octopus to resemble crab meat. Tenderized octopus is also delicious pickled.

Octopus is relatively low in calories (70 gm per 100 gm) and is a good source of protein (14.6 gm per 100 gm).

CRABS
Order Decapoda

Life History

Because it has a hard shell, the crab cannot grow unless it sheds its shell. Before the crab sheds, it forms a new, soft shell under the old shell. The old shell splits and the crab backs out of it. The new, soft shell expands as the crab takes in large amounts of water. The crab is very vulnerable to predation right after molting, so it tends to seek protection. Within a day the shell is relatively hard. The body fluids in the new, larger shell are gradually replaced by muscle as the crab feeds. Young crabs molt often, but adult crabs generally molt only once a year.

Mating usually takes place soon after the female has molted. The male transfers the sperm to the female. When the eggs mature, they are fertilized by the sperm and stored under the female's abdomen. After hatching, the pelagic larvae go through several planktonic stages before taking on their adult form.

Crabs have the unusual ability to regenerate legs. This adaptation is believed to help get rid of an injured leg or to escape from predators. During the molt after loss of the limb, a new leg is produced. It takes several molts for the leg to grow back to normal size.

The dungeness crab, *Cancer magister*, is typical of the group of crabs called Cancer crabs. *Cancer magister* is common from central California to Alaska in waters less than 300 ft deep. The males fertilize freshly molted females during spring and the females each extrude 750,000 to 2,500,000 eggs during the following fall. The eggs hatch within a couple of months and the larvae metamorphosize into the bottom-dwelling adult form about 4 months later. They grow to sexual maturity at 4 inches and reach legal size in 3.5 to 4 years. The males grow to larger sizes than females, with a maximum width of 9 inches at an age of 6 years. They feed on fish, juvenile crabs, clams, and small crustaceans.

The huge king crab, *Paralithodes camtschatica*, is closely related to the tiny hermit crab. King crabs migrate to nearshore waters to breed during spring. The eggs are fertilized during the female's molt and she carries them for 11 months. After mating the crabs return to deeper waters (600-900 ft). After a 2- or 3-month pelagic larval period, the young crabs settle down to the bottom. They grow to sexual maturity in 6 years. They grow up to 25 lb in size. King crabs are found primarily in Alaskan waters.

Another group of crabs, spider crabs, has received increased attention in recent years by researchers and fishermen. The crabs of the genus *Chionoecetes*, in the spider crab group, are known as tanner or snow crabs. They are most common in Alaskan waters. They are smaller than king crabs, reaching approximately 5 lb. Tanner crabs are long-lived (up to 15 years) and have reproductive histories similar to those of king crabs.

Fishery Information

Large, valuable fisheries exist for crab along the Pacific Coast. The dungeness crab fishery developed during the 1920s. The landings fluctuate widely with catches well above 30,000,000 lb during good years. There appears to be a cyclical pattern to crab abundance. The cause of these cycles is unclear. Some of the alternative explanations include the intensity of upwelling, water temperature variations, cannibalism, and predation. The central California population still has not recovered from the last down cycle, during the mid-1960s.

Cylindrical traps baited with fish, clams,or squid are used to catch dungeness crabs. Vessels run 100 to 500 traps per day. Only the male crabs, which are larger than the females, are taken. It is estimated that 90% of the legal-sized males are captured each year. The season starts in the late fall and peaks during the winter. In Alaska most catches occur during the summer.

Closely related *Cancer* crabs are fished in the nearshore waters of central and southern California. The fishery has grown dramatically in the last 10 years, with over 1,000,000 lb landed annually. Three species, the rock crab (*Cancer antennarius*), the yellow crab (*C. anthonyi*), and the red crab (*C. productus*), are landed with lighter, rectangular traps. A significant recreational fishery also exists for these species.

The modern Alaska king crab fishery developed in the early 1950s. By 1966 the landings reached 159,000,000 lb, but slumped to 88,000,000 lb by 1981 and there is now concern for the economic viability of the fishery.

Large steel vessels make up the bulk of the fleet. The vessels must be able to handle large numbers of 8 ft x 8 ft traps that each weigh 700 to 800 lb. Many of the vessels have live tanks to hold the crabs until they reach the processor. Crab must be processed live for best quality. Rugged weather, high risk, and high potential earnings characterize this fishery.

As king crab catches began to decline in the late 1960s, interest grew in the tanner or snow crabs off Alaska. The fishery has grown from 118,000 lb in 1967 to over 100,000,000 lb today. This crab is similar in appearance to king crab, only much smaller.

Consumer Information

Like many other seafoods, crabs are high in protein and low in fat (0.7 to 1.4 gm of fat per 100 gm). Dungeness crab is also relatively low in calories (85 calories per 100 gm).

Dungeness crabs are available live or fresh cooked during the season, which runs from mid-November until summer. The majority are landed during December and January. Dungeness crabs are landed from San Francisco to Alaska. Some of the crabs are pickled or the meat is available fresh, frozen, or canned. Approximately 20% to 25% of the live weight of the crab is meat. During the closed season, cooked frozen crabs and crab meat are available. Often large rubber bands are used on frozen whole crabs to keep their legs in place. The price of dungeness crab varies widely from year to year due to large changes in availability.

King and snow crab are usually sold as frozen sections. At times markets in Seattle and Alaska will have fresh king and snow crab legs. Recently several companies have begun to market imitation king crab legs made with extruded fish flesh ("surimi"), crab flavoring, and coloring.

The rock crabs are marketed primarily in southern California.

They are available most of the year live or cooked whole. Sometimes just the claws are marketed.

If you catch or buy live crabs, they should be cooked live in boiling water. Cook dungeness crabs approximately 20 minutes. Uncooked dead crabs are highly perishable.

SHRIMPS
Order Decapoda

Life History

Shrimps are closely related to crabs and lobsters. There are at least 85 species of shrimp found along the Pacific Coast. Most of the economically important species are in the family Pandalidae.

Pandalid shrimp mate in the fall and the female extrudes several thousand eggs. The eggs hatch the following spring and the pelagic larval stage lasts about 3 months. Shrimp generally are hermaphroditic, maturing within 18 months as males. They function as males for 1 or 2 years before transforming into females. The percentage of shrimp changing sex is highly variable. The strength of each year class is also highly variable, probably due to variable survival rates of larval shrimp. Some feel that the abundance of predators, such as hake, *Merluccius productus*, has a significant effect on shrimp populations.

Fishery Information

The major Pacific Coast shrimp fisheries harvest two relatively small species, the northern pink shrimp, *Pandalus borealis*, and the ocean pink shrimp, *Pandalus jordani*. The northern pink shrimp is the major species harvested in Alaska. In many years over 100,000,000 lb are landed. This shrimp is important commerically in the north Atlantic also. The pink shrimp provides a large fishery in Washington, Oregon, and California with landings in some years of over 75,000,000 lb.

Trawlers using small meshed shrimp trawls land these valuable shrimp. Because of the great variation in year class strength, the amount caught fluctuates widely from year to year. Good fishing in the late 1970s attracted many boats to the fishery, but these fishermen fell on hard times when weaker year classes lowered catches in 1981 and 1982.

Trawlers and trap fishermen are targeting on a group of larger pandalid shrimp along the entire coast. Although the landings are relatively small, these large shrimp bring a high price. The spot shrimp, *Pandalus platyceros*, reaches a length of 9 inches. They tend to be near submarine canyons or other locales with adequate hiding places. In a few locations, such as near Santa Barbara, there are enough spot shrimp available over trawling grounds to justify a fishery. Spot shrimp and coonstripe shrimp, *Pandalus hysinotus*, are often a valuable incidental catch for trawlers. Recreational fishermen from Puget Sound northward also trap these shrimp in 100- to 400-ft depths

A group of small bay shrimp of the genus *Crago* are important as forage and bait in some bays. There is a small and successful bait fishery in San Francisco Bay for *Crago*. They are sold at a high price as bait for sturgeon, striped bass, and perch. Although landings are low now, Chinese fishermen used to land 3,000,000 lb annually (1929 and 1935), which were dried and exported.

A non-pandalid shrimp fishery for the ridgeback prawn, *Eusicyonia ingentis*, has developed in the Santa Barbara Channel. Trawlers are making sizable landings and biological studies are currently being conducted to determine how the resource should be managed.

Consumer Information

Unlike the large shrimp (family Penaeidae) landed in the Gulf of Mexico, Pacific shrimp are mostly small. The bulk of the northern and ocean pink shrimp are processed by peeling machines and marketed fresh or frozen as cocktail shrimp. Larger but less common shrimp, such as the spot shrimp, are marketed and prepared much like shrimp from the Gulf of Mexico.

Both the Mexican shrimp and the smaller Pacific Coast shrimp are available frozen or thrawed all year. The Pacific shrimp are most abundant during the spring and summer months. Many of them are frozen in 1- and 5-lb cans. Shrimp are rarely marketed fresh because they are highly perishable.

The most popular way to cook raw shrimp is to boil them in sea water or salted fresh water (¼ cup salt per quart) for 3 to 8 minutes, depending on the size of the shrimp. After they cool, the shrimp can be shelled. Shrimp tend to be high in protein and cholesterol, but low in fat and calories.

GYOTAKU MATERIALS AND METHODS

A Little History

"Gyotaku" (pronounced ghio-ta-koo) means fish rubbing (gyo = fish, taku = rubbing). Fish rubbing or fish printing is a relatively new art form; it is believed to have originated in Japan in the mid-1800s. The oldest existing "gyotaku" is of a red sea bream done for Lord Sakai in 1862. In Japan the art form has been used primarily to record anglers' catch. Fishermen may stretch the truth, but fish prints don't lie!

"Gyotaku" developed relatively slowly in Japan until the 1950s when the artists formed "Gyotaku-no-kai," the "Gyotaku" Association. The sharing of techniques and ideas accelerated the development of "gyotaku." The Japanese are masters of both the direct and indirect printing methods.

The first expert American fish printer was Mrs. John Roemhild Canning, an illustrator of fishes with the Smithsonian Institution. Her unique combination of illustration skills and knowledge about fish enabled her to introduce many American to "gyotaku." Mrs. Canning worked closely with the head of "Gyotaku-no-kai," Dr. Yoshio Hiyama, from the University of Tokyo. The works of the Japanese "gyotaku" masters were displayed at the American Museum of Natural History in New York in 1956. Years later Mrs. Canning was honored by having her fish prints exhibited in Tokyo with the "Gyotaku-no-kai" members in their annual show.

In 1964, with Mrs. Canning's assistance, the University of Washington Press published Dr. Hiyama's book, *Gyotaku—the Art and Technique of the Japanese Fish Print*. This excellent book was the first in-depth work in English about fish printing. Scores of American artists and naturalists, including myself, used this book to learn basic "gyotaku" techniques. We all had to adapt the Japanese techniques to utilize materials available in the United States.

At the same time that "gyotaku" was being discoved by Americans, the closely related art of plant printing was reborn, chiefly through the enthusiasm and energy of botanist Robert Little in Pennsylvania. Plant printing developed in Europe in the 1400s. Leonardo da Vinci was one of the earliest plant printers and Benjamin Franklin used plant prints on Colonial currency. Many of the great botanical books of Europe during the 18th and 10th centuries were illustrated with prints.

In 1976 fish and plant printers formed the U.S. Nature Printing Society. This society has brought about a tremendous expansion of these art forms through exhibits, classes, and publications. In 1981 the Nature Printing Society, the Santa Barbara Museum of Natural History, and the Smithsonian Museum of Natural History organized the most comprehensive collection of "gyotaku" and plant prints ever assembled in the United States. The exhibition traveled to dozens of museums throughout the United States and Canada between 1981 and 1984.

Materials

You will need a few basic materials to make a fish print. Fish, ink, paper, brushes, and plastic modeling clay are essential.

Fish obviously are critical. Fresh fish are best. If you catch the fish yourself, either keep it alive until you are ready to print or kill it immediately and keep it cool. Generally, if I can't print a fish within 36 hours of capture, I freeze it for later use. Frozen fish don't work as well, but they often are your only choice. Be sure to protect the fins and body of the fish from damage. Any loss of scales, cuts, or torn fins will show in your "gyotaku." You may gut the fish and then stuff the body cavity with paper towels to recreate the original body shape. I do this often with prized food fish such as salmon.

Beginning printers should start with relatively small (6- to 18-inch), flat-bodied fish with large scales and spines. Some good choices are rockfish, perch, bluegill, and flounder. Round and delicate fish such as tuna and trout are extremely difficult.

If you buy whole fish from a market, make sure fins and body are in good shape. Look for freshness, because the fine detail of the fish gradually disappears as the fish decomposes. Fresh fish usually have red gills, clear and non-sunken eyes, and little or no fishy odor. Obtaining a good fish is a key to producing successfuly "gyotaku."

One of the most enjoyable parts of fish printing is testing and learning about papers. Handmade papers, called "washi" by the Japanese, are preferred. These papers are made throughout the world, but the Japanese and Chinese make the best papers for "gyotaku." Papers have been highly prized in Oriental cultures for years.

They are used for gifts, art, clothing, housing, and decoration.

These papers are often incorrectly called "rice paper." The papers are actually made from the inner bark of trees such as the paper mulberry (kozo) tree. The long fibers of the bark are separated and suspended in water, sometimes with pounded *Hibiscus* root for sizing. The skilled paper maker uses a bamboo screen which is dipped into and removed from the vat of suspended fibers. Each thin layer of 5- to-10-mm long fibers forms a single sheet of paper (typical wood pulp papers have fibers less than 1 mm long). The long fibers give the hand-made papers the strength and moisture tolerance necessary for "gyotaku."

There are hundreds of papers available. The names are some-what confusing. Some papers are named after the maker ("Abe"), some after the raw material ("kozo"), and others after the locality ("mino," the old name of Gifu prefecture). Individual fish printers seem to have their own favorite papers. Generally one looks for a flexible, strong, moisture-absorbent paper. My favorites are "Abe," "kumoi," "kozo," "chauke," "mino-buff" and "goyu." Some fish printers, when using oil-base inks, use heavier papers such as "torinoko" which they soak in water until flexible enough for printing.

Because of the expense of handmade paper ($.80 to $10 per sheet), beginning printers should start with newsprint or "sumi-e" sketching paper. I always use newsprint for the first couple of prints until I'm sure the fish is ready to produce satisfactory prints. One should experiment with several different papers. I do this by buying single sheets and by printing directly on the sample paper books available from large paper suppliers. Whenever I'm in a new city, I try to locate Oriental art stores that might carry unique papers.

Fish Anatomy

To create good "gyotaku" it is useful to understand fish anatomy. Most fish have at least one dorsal fin, a tail fin, an anal fin, a pair of ventral fins, and a pair of pectoral fins. Often the first dorsal fin will have hard, sharp spines, while the other fins will have soft, flexible fin rays. The spines and rays are connected by thin, fleshy skin that readily collects excess mucus and ink that should be wiped off after each print. Some fish, such as trout and salmon, have a small, fleshy adipose fin that is difficult, but important, to print.

Here is a rough sketch of external fish anatomy:

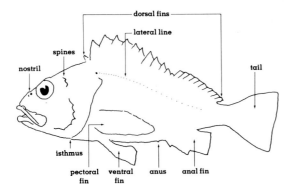

Fish scales vary in structure. Sharks have sandpaper-like scales that are really modified teeth; they are difficult to print and require an extra thick coating of ink. Trout, salmon, and smelt have delicate "deciduous" scales that are difficult to print; sometimes removing all scales and printing the scale pockets that the fish lie in is best. Many fish have hard, rough scales (i.e. perch, rockfish); their scales will turn out well in prints, and these fish are the easiest to work with.

Most fish have at least one lateral line. The lateral line is a series of small organs used by the fish to sense turbulence and pressure changes. If you print correctly, the lateral line will be very striking in your prints. Many fish have spines around the head. If properly printed, most of the fish's spines will reproduced beautifully.

Fish secrete mucus from their bodies to protect themselves from parasites and disease and to help them "slip" through the water easily. The mucus tends to make a fish print less clearly and appear dark in color. For this reason it is important to remove as much mucus as possible by washing the fish thoroughly. Mucus tends to collect on the fins, near the anus, gill cover, isthumus and nostrils, and under the pectoral fins.

Fishes' bodies vary greatly in shape. A flat flounder lies on the ocean bottom, while a round, bullet-shaped tuna needs to swim efficiently to capture prey. Generally, the flatter the fish, the easier it is to print.

The Direct Method

The most important step in fish printing is preparation of the fish. The surface of the fish must be thoroughly cleaned because mucus and dirt will obscure the exquisite detail. Wash the fish in soap (e.g. dish detergent, Boraxo) and water until the mucus is gone. Salt or baking soda can also be used. Be careful not to remove any scales or damage the fins. Areas with missing scales will show up with a much different texture on your print. Fish with easily removed, deciduous scales, such as salmon and trout, can be scaled completely before printing.

Dry the fish off completely and place it on a newspaper-covered table. Moisture will obscure the detail so you should meticulously and continuously dry off the mouth, nostrils, fins, gills, and other moisture-collecting areas. You should plug the anus of the fish with a small piece of paper towel or cotton to prevent it from leaking onto your printing paper. Keep the fish out of direct sunlight because the fins will dry out too fast and the water-based ink may dry before you make your "gyotaku."

Form the plastic modeling clay into a shape similar to each of the fins. Position the fins in a natural pose and place the clay underneath the fins for support. Straight pins can be used to hold the fins in place. Whenever possible, I try to avoid the use of pins because they damage the fins and show up on the print.

Now you are ready to print (Figure 1). Using a stiff ½ to 1-inch brush, apply a thin coat of ink. Apply the ink from the head toward the tail, doing the fins last (Figure 2). When applying the ink to the fins, hold a piece of paper along the margin of the fins so you won't slop ink onto the clay. Leave the eye blank; you will paint this in later. After removing excess ink from your brush, brush firmly from the tail toward the head (Figure 3). This will catch the ink along the edge of the scales and spines, producing sharper detail.

Carefully place your paper over the top of the fish. I always use a piece of newsprint for the first print to remove the remaining mucus and to experiment. Starting at the head, press the paper firmly with your fingers over the entire inked fish (Figure 4). Be careful not to move or wrinkle the paper excessively. With round-bodied fish you will have to move the paper somewhat to avoid wrinkles. Try to minimize the paper movement to avoid blurred or double impressions on

1. A fish is ready for direct printing after it has been washed, dried off, and the fins supported with clay.

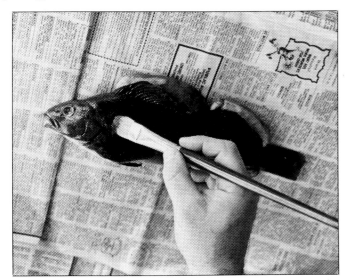

2. Brush a thin coat of ink on the fish, brushing from the head toward the tail.

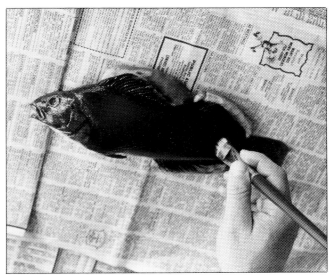

3. For a clear print, the final brush strokes should be made from the tail toward the head.

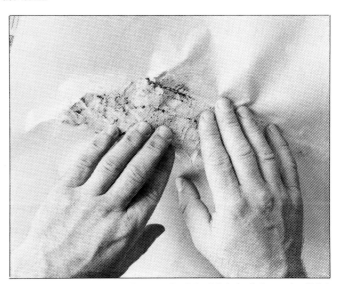

4. The paper is placed carefully over the inked fish and the entire fish is then rubbed with your fingers to transfer the ink to the paper.

Fish printing photos by Christine Marshall Dewees.

5. Carefully remove the paper and let it dry. Then the eye may be painted in by hand.

some parts of the fish. After the paper has been pressed down on the entire inked fish, remove the paper and look for ways to improve the next print (Figure 5). The fish can then be re-inked and the entire process repeated. You should be able to get 5 to 10 prints from a fish.

The next step is to carefully paint in the eye with a small brush. Look closely at the fish's eye and note the size and colors of the eye. The fish can now be washed off, filleted, and prepared for dinner.

I often work with only black ink, but many fish printers prefer using other colors. It is a challenge to try to duplicate the natural coloration and counter-shading (dark on top, light below) of the fish. Use a different brush for each color. I usually apply the lightest colors first. A natural-looking transition between colors is critical. Just before printing I use a soft brush to smooth the area where different colors meet.

Composition is also important. Try to give the fish some motion by curving the fins and placing the fish at an angle. Schools of fish are effective. Different-colored fish or different ink intensities can give the impression of depth. Try to use different-sized fish rather than repeating the same fish over and over. Overlap fish by masking off part of the fish in the background. Print the fish around other printed objects such as seaweed, lily pads, driftwood, and rocks. Use your imagination.

Directing Printing with Brayers

Some fish printers use soft rubber brayers (rollers) instead of brushes to apply the ink. Brayers are used in block printing and for making plant prints. The size of the brayer used depends on the size of the fish; in general, 1- to 4-inch brayers are used. I use this technique with fish that are quite slick and have little relief such as rays, skates, salmon, and flounders. The brayer eliminates problems with brush strokes. Some American fish printers, especially those who first learned European plant printing techniques, use brayers for all of their fish prints.

The fish is prepared in exactly the same manner as for the direct method. The same materials are used except for the brayer and a heavy sheet of glass (12 inches x 18 inches or larger). A fish, such as a skate, is placed on newspaper. The ink is rolled out with the brayer on the glass until the brayer is thinly covered. Then the ink is rolled onto the fish with the brayer. Be sure to roll on the ink in the same direction over the entire fish. After inking, the fish is moved to a clean surface and a direct print is made.

I stick to water-based inks with this method, but other artists use oil-based inks successfully. By layering different colors with different viscosities of ink some interesting effects are obtained. Plants are successfully printed using this technique also. This method brings together the Japanese "gyotaku" methods with European plant printing techniques to create a uniquely American style. With the use of brayers I usually cannot obtain the fine detail of a traditional direct method print, but I can achieve many pleasing color and textural effects.

Indirect Method

The direct method is relatively simple to learn, although mastery takes years of practice. The indirect method is more time consuming, exacting, and difficult to learn. While few Americans have mastered the indirect method, it is the dominant technique used by the Japanese masters today. Even in Japan, fish printers tend to master only the direct or indirect method; few can do both well.

The major difference between the direct and indirect methods is that with the indirect method, one molds the paper to the fish and then applies the ink to the paper. Startling physical detail and color can be achieved with this method. The indirect method is difficult to describe and each person must develop and practice his own technique.

Several different materials are required. The paper used must be very thin and transparent, yet strong when moist. "Gampi," "gasen," and "mino" are the papers preferred by the Japanese. I've had my best luck with "Abe" paper. You will also need to make some tampos of different sizes (¼- to 1-inch). These are made by tightly wrapping cotton inside a piece of fine silk or cotton cloth. The finished tampo should look like an upside-down mushroom. The tampo is used to apply the ink.

Prepare the fish exactly as you would for a direct print. Be especially sure to remove all mucus and blood from the fish. Place the printing paper over the top of the fish. Then place a thin, moist rag over the paper or mist the paper with water using a spray bottle. Let the paper soak up the moisture for a few minutes. Then carefully and slowly mold the paper to the fish. Don't force the paper or it will tear. Press the paper to the fish as if you were doing a direct fish print.

After attaching the paper to the fish, it must be left to dry. The length of drying time varies and practice is the only way to learn. The drier the paper, the sharper the detail in the print. But if the paper dries too much, the paper will come loose from the fish and the ink will not be absorbed well enough. If the air is humid, an electric hair dryer can be used to dry the paper quickly.

You are now ready to apply the ink with the tampos. Dip the tampos into the ink and then use a test paper (slightly less absorbent than the printing paper) to test the amount of ink on the tampo. Apply the ink with light brushing strokes of the tampo, parallel to the fish's surface. Don't just blot the ink onto the paper.

Apply the lightest colors first. Small tampos, attached to the eraser end of a pencil, can be used to bring out details such as the mouth and spines. When doing the fins, a piece of paper should be placed along the margin of the fins to prevent the ink from diffusing out into the paper.

The next problem is removing the completed print from the fish. This again takes patience. If the paper is stuck hard to the fish, apply moisture with a brush to the *underside* of the fins. (If you apply water to the paper, the print will run.) After applying the water, wait a few minutes for the moisture to soak through the fins. The paper will then be easier to remove. Start at the tail and work carefully toward the head.

The indirect method takes patience, practice, and judgment; but the results are worthwhile. Dr. Hiyama's books listed at the end of the book give the best description of and instructions for making indirect "gyotaku."

Care of Fish Prints

Once you're created a number of "gyotaku," you will need to store and/or display them. Here are a few ideas I've come across.

If possible, store the prints and papers flat in drawers and/or folders. Keep them dry and as bug-free as possible. If you don't have room, the fish prints and papers can be rolled up. However, during the process of rolling and transporting the prints, they inevitably will become wrinkled.

In addition to the wrinkles caused by handling, the process of fish printing stretches the paper and creates wrinkles. If these imperfections bother you, they can be lessened by several methods. The entire back of the paper with the fish print on it can be misted with water from a spray bottle. Don't use too much water or the print will run. The paper is then placed between two acid-free blotters and the blotters are then pressed down with an even weight (glass or wood) for several hours. Change blotters several times until the paper is dry. This will take most wrinkles out. Other methods involve mounting the print on another handmade paper use rice paste or a low-temperature mounting material called thermoplast. A professional art preserver should be consulted in using these methods. Avoid dry mounting processes such as those used for photographs because the wrinkles in the paper will be transformed into permanent creases when dry mounted.

"Gyotaku" can be matted and framed like any other art on **paper. If you want your fish prints to outlive you, acid-free (pH neutral)** mounting and matting materials should be used.

Some Sources of Materials for Printing

Papers and Art Supplies

Aiko's Art Materials Import
714 N. Wabash Avenue
Chicago, IL 60611

Andrews-Nelson-Whitehead
3110 48th Avenue
Long Island City, NY 11101

Ashe Artist Materials
Venice Studio Village
608 Venice Boulevard
Venice, CA 90291

Aya's
3434 Atlantic Avenue
Long Beach, CA 90807

China Cultural Center
210 Mandarin Place
Los Angeles, CA 90012

Flax
10852 Lindbrook Drive
West Los Angeles, CA 90024

Cando Hoshino
1541 Clement Street
San Francisco, CA 94118

Japan Folk Art
147 Monte Rey Drive S.
Los Alamas, NM 87544

Kensington Paper Mill
2527 Magnolia
Oakland, CA 94607

Guy T. Kuhn, Fine Art Papers
Box 166
Keedysville, MD 21756

McManus and Morgan
2506 W. 7th Street
Los Angeles, CA 90057

New York Central Supply Co.
63 Third Avenue
New York, NY 10003

Rice Paper Specialists
P.O. Box 1425
San Bruno, CA 94066

Daniel Smith, Inc.
1111 West Nickerson Street
Seattle, WA 98119

Taiwan Handmade Paper
  Manufacturing Co., Ltd.
47-3 Chang-An West Road
Taipei, 102, Taiwan

Yasutomo and Company
24 California Street
San Francisco, CA 94111

Inks and Art Supplies

Faust Engraving Inks
542 South Avenue
East Cranford, NJ 07016

Gano Ink and Supply Co.
1441 Boyd Street
Los Angeles, CA 90033

Graphic Chemical and Ink Co.
728 North Yale Avenue
Villa Park, IL 60181

Inmont Corp.
1133 Avenue of the Americas
New York, NY 10036

Kelsey Co.
Box 941
Meriden, CT 06540

Daniel Smith, Inc.
1111 W. Nickerson Street
Seattle, WA 98119

Glossary

Adipose fin Small, fleshy dorsal fin found in front of the tail. A distinguishing characteristic of the salmon and smelt families.

Amphipod A small, insect-like crustacean. Beach-hoppers found under rotting seaweed are amphipods.

Anadromous fish Fish that spawn in fresh water and live part of their life in marine water.

Anal fin Fin located just behind the anus on the underside of fish.

Aquaculture Rearing of aquatic organisms in a controlled environment.

Cast net A small circular net used to catch small fish. The net is thrown over the top of a school of fish and then closed by pulling on a line like a purse string.

Community An association of interacting populations, usually defined by their interactions or by spatial occurrence.

Copepods Small, planktonic crustaceans that are important food for small, pelagic fishes.

Cultch Substrate used for attachment by bivalve mollusks (oysters, mussels) when they first settle out of the plankton. Often shells are used.

Demersal fishes Fishes associated with the bottom rather than the open ocean.

Dorsal fin(s) Fin(s) located on the top side of the fish.

Eel grass A flowering plant, *Zostera* sp., that grows in protected bays. It is an important food for many birds and estuarine organisms.

Estuary Body of water where a river empties into the ocean (bay).

Euphausiids Small, pelagic, shrimp-like crustaceans that are important food for many midwater fishes.

Fecundity The number of mature eggs or embryos produced; potential reproductive capacity. Usually expressed only for females.

Habitat types Place where organisms live, such as sandy beaches or rocky reefs.

Hermaphrodite Life history strategy of an organism which changes from one sex to another during its life span.

Intertidal zone Area between the extremes of high and low tide.

Isthumus Narrow extension of the fish's throat and gill chambers.

Kelp General name for large, brown seaweed which form large "beds" off our shores. Usually *Macrocystis* sp. or *Nereocystis* sp.

Lampara A large, surrounding net similar to a purse seine (see gear illustrations) but lacking the bottom-closing ability of a purse seine. Used in the squid fishery.

Lateral line Row of pore-like openings, usually along the side of the fish's body, used to sense turbulence and pressure changes.

Maximum sustainable yield Largest average catch which can continuously be taken from a stock without harming the stock. When modified by socioeconomic factors, it is called the optimum sustainable yield.

Menhaden Herring-like fishes of the genus *Brevoortia*. Huge quantities are captured in the Gulf of Mexico and off the Atlantic Coast. Menhaden are processed into fish meal and oil.

Midwater trawler A large (usually over 60 ft), powerful fishing vessel that pulls a large trawl net (see gear illustrations) above the bottom rather than on the bottom. Fish such as hake and widow rockfish are captured.

Mooching Fishing techniques used by anglers to catch salmon. Involves slowly raising and lowering a baited hook while drifting in a boat.

Nursery Any area utilized by juvenile animals for feeding and protection.

Paralytic shellfish poisoning	Poisoning in humans caused by the eating of bivalve mollusks which have high concentrations of toxic *Gonyaulax catenella* plankton.
Pelagic fishes	Fishes that are associated with the open ocean rather than the bottom or shore.
Plankton	Small (usually microscopic), aquatic plants and animals.
Population	Groups of individuals of any one kind of organism.
Recruitment	Addition of new fish to the population vulnerable to fishing by growth from smaller sizes.
Roe	Fish eggs.
Speciation	The process of forming a population or group of distinct organisms (species) that have common characteristics and are reproductively isolated from other distinct organisms.
Thermocline	The layer of water in which rapid temperature change takes place, usually between the upper, sun-warmed water layer and the lower, cold-water layer.
Trammel net	An entangling net similar to a gill net (see gear illustrations) except a trammel has several layers of netting.
Upwelling	Vertical movement of water currents, usually near coasts and driven by onshore winds, that brings nutrients from the depths of the oceans to surface layers.
Year class	Group of organims that were born in the same year.
Zooplankton	Small aquatic animals that are important food for fish and shellfish.

Fishing Gear Illustrations[1]

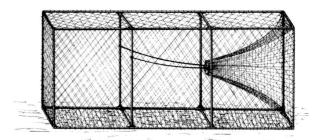

1. Fish Trap (Sablefish)

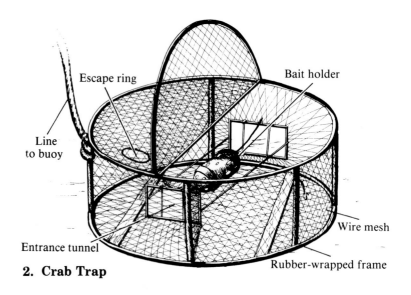

2. Crab Trap

[1]Illustrations from:

Austin, S. V. 1981. *A Guide to Oregon's Commercial Fishing Vessels.* Oregon State University Sea Grant Leaflet 68.

Dewees, C. M. and J. K. Hooper. 1976. *Major Commercial Fisheries in California.* University of California Ag. Sciences leaflet 2272.

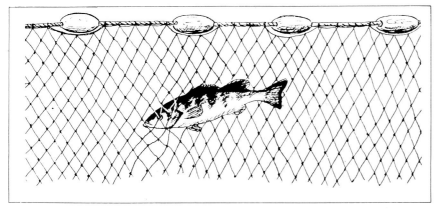

3. Gillnet

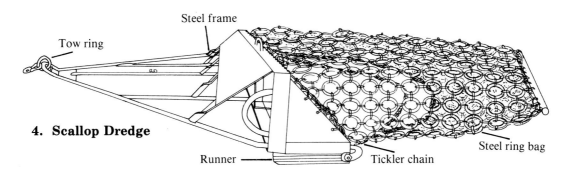

4. Scallop Dredge

Tow ring

Steel frame

Runner

Tickler chain

Steel ring bag

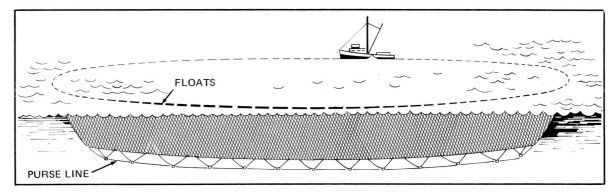

FLOATS

PURSE LINE

5. Purse Seine

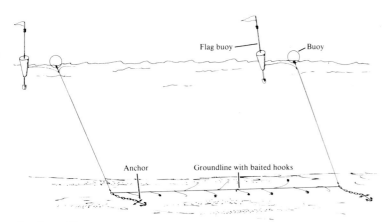

6. Longline

Flag buoy

Buoy

Anchor

Groundline with baited hooks

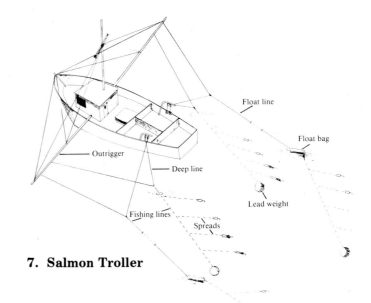

7. Salmon Troller

Float line

Float bag

Outrigger

Deep line

Lead weight

Fishing lines

Spreads

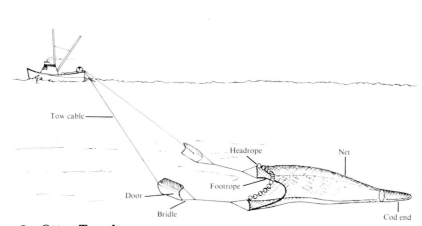

8. Otter Trawl

Tow cable

Headrope

Net

Footrope

Door

Bridle

Cod end

General References on
Pacific Coast Fishes and Fisheries

Austin. S. V. 1981. *A Guide to Oregon's Commercial Fishing Vessels.* Oregon State Univ., Corvallis, OR. Sea Grant Leafl. 68. 12 pp.

Barrett, E. M. 1963. *The California Oyster Industry.* Calif. Dep. Fish Fish and Game, Fish Bull., (123):1-103.

Baxter, J. L. (Revised by J. M. Duffy). 1974. *Inshore Fisheries of California.* Calif. Dep. Fish and Game, Sacramento, CA. 78 pp.

Bell, F. H. 1981. *The Pacific Halibut.* Alaska Northwest Publ., Anchorage, AK. 267 pp.

Browning, R. J. 1980. *Fisheries of the North Pacific.* Northwest Publ., Anchorage, AK. 432 pp.

Bulter, T. H. 1980. *Shrimps of the Pacific Coast of Canada.* Canadian Dep. Fish. and Oceans, Bull., (202):1-280.

Caldwell, F. E. 1978. *Pacific Troller.* Alaska Northwest Publ., Anchorage, AK. 143 pp.

Cannon, R. 1953. *Fishing the Pacific Coast.* Lane Publ., Menlo Park, CA. 337 pp.

Davis, C. 1977. *Hook Up—A Complete Guide to Southern California Ocean Sportfishing.* Outdoor Empire Publ., Seattle, WA. 177 pp.

Dehlendorf, S. 1981. *Anchovy: Little Fish, Big Dispute.* Pacific Fishing 2(10):56-59.

Dewees, C. M. 1976. *Catching, Cook and Cleaning Crabs.* Univ. of Calif. Agric. Sci., Leafl. (2546):1-2.

————. 1980. *The Sablefish Fishery.* Univ. of Calif. Agric. Sci., Leafl. (21155):1-10.

Dewees, C. M., and R. J. Price. 1983. *The California Squid Fishery.* Univ. Calif. Agric. Sci., Leafl. (21330):1-14.

Eschmeyer, W. M., E. S. Herald, and H. Hammann. 1983. *A Field Guide to Pacific Coast Fishes of North America.* Houghton Mifflin, Boston, MD. 336 pp.

Feinberg, L., and T. Morgan. 1980. *California's Salmon Resource— Its Biology, Use and Management.* Univ. of Calif. Sea Grant Coll. Program, La Jolla, CA. 38 pp.

Fitch, J. E. 1953. *Common Marine Bivalves of California.* Calif. Dep. Fish and Game, Fish Bull., (90):1-102.

————. 1969. *Offshore Fishes of California.* Calif. Dep. Fish and Game, Sacramento, CA. 80 pp.

Fitch, J. E., and R. J. Lavenberg. 1975. *Deep-Water Fishes of California.* Univ. of Calif. Press, Berkeley, CA. 155 pp.

————. 1971. *Marine Food and Game Fishes of California.* Univ. of Calif. Press, Berkeley, CA. 179 pp.

————. 1975. *Tidepool and Nearshore Fishes of California.* Univ. of Calif. Press, Berkeley, CA 156 pp.

Frey, H. W. (Editor). 1971. *California's Living Marine Resources and Their Utilization.* Calif. Dep. Fish and Game, Sacramento, CA. 148 pp.

Gotshall, D. W. 1981. *Pacific Coast Inshore Fishes.* Sea Challengers, Los Osos, CA. 96 pp.

Hart, J. L. 1973. *Pacific Fishes of Canada.* Fish. Res. Bd. Can., Ottawa. 740 pp.

Herald, E. S. 1961. *Living Fishes of the World.* Hamish Hamilton Ltd., London. 304 pp.

Higgins, J. 1978. *The North Pacific Deckhands' and Alaska Cannery Workers' Handbook.* Albacore Press, Eastsound, WA. 91 pp.

Joseph, J., W. Klawe, and P. Murphy. 1980. *Tuna and Billfish—Fish Without a Country.* Inter-Amer. Trop. Tuna Comm., La Jolla, CA. 46 pp.

Marshall, N. B. 1966. *The Life of Fishes.* Universe Books, New York, NY. 402 pp.

Maxwell, W. D. 1975. *The Croakers of California.* Calif. Dep. Fish and Game, Marine Resour. Leafl., (119):1-16.

Miller, D. J., and R. N. Lea. 1972. *Guide to the Coastal Marine Fishes of California.* Calif. Dep. Fish and Game, Fish Bull., (157):1-249.

Moyle, P. B., and J. J. Cech, Jr. 1982. *Fishes—An Introduction to Ichthyology.* Prentice-Hall, Englewood Cliffs, NJ. 593 pp.

Orbach, M. K. 1977. *Hunters, Seamen, and Entrepreneurs—The Tuna Seinemen of San Diego.* Univ. of Calif. Press, Berkeley, CA. 304 pp.

Phillips, J. B. 1973. *California Market Crab and Its Close Relatives.* Calif. Dep. Fish and Game, Marine Resourc. Leafl. (5):1-14.

Radovich, J. 1970. *How to Catch, Bone and Cook a Shad.* Calif. Dep. Fish and Game, Sacramento, CA. 43 pp.

Robins, C. R. (Chairman). 1980. *A List of Common and Scientific Names of Fishes From the United States and Canada.* (4th edition) American Fisheries Society, Bethesda, MD. Spec. Pub. 12. 174 pp.

Schultz, L. P. 1936. *Keys to the Fishes of Washington, Oregon and Closely Adjoining Regions.* Univ. of Wash. Publ. in Biol. 2(4):103-228.

Squire, J. L., and S. E. Smith. 1977. *Anglers' Guide to the Unite States Pacific Coast.* Natl. Mar. Fish. Serv., Washington, D.C. 139 pp.

Stansby, M. E. 1976. *Chemical Characteristics of Fish Caught in the Northeast Pacific Ocean.* Mar. Fish. Rev. 38(9):1-11.

Thomson, D. A., L. T. Finley, and A. N. Kerstitch. 1979. *Reef Fishes of the Sea of Cortez.* John Wiley, New York, NY. 302 pp.

Turner, G. H., and J. C. Sexsmith. 1967. *Marine Baits of California.* Calif. Dep. Fish and Game, Sacramento, CA. 71 pp.

Walford, L. A. 1974. *Marine Game Fishes of the Pacific Coast From Alaska to the Equator.* T.F.H. Publications, Neptune, NJ. 205 pp.

"Gyotaku" References

Cave, R. and G. Wakeman. 1967. *Typographia Naturalis: A History of Nature Printing.* Brewhouse Press: Wymondham, England.

Dewees, C.M. 1981. *Gyotaku—Japanese Fish Printing.* University of California Ag. Sci. Leaflet 2548.

————. 1981. *When Nature Becomes Art.* International Wildlife. 11(5):36-39.

————. 1984. *Gyotaku-Catching Fish on Paper.* Oceans. 17(4): 40-43.

Fisher, J. 1977. *Wildlife Omnibus: How to Master Gyotaku.* International Wildlife. 7(1):18-19.

Geary, I. 1978. *Plant Prints and Collages.* Viking Press: New York.

Hiyama, Y. 1955. *Gyotaku.* Japan Quarterly. 2(2):210-213.

————. 1964. *Gyotaku. The Art and Technique of the Japanese Fish Print.* University of Washington Press: Seattle.

————. 1972. *Gyotaku. An Art of Fish Print.* Kodansha: Tokyo.

Hochberg, F. G. 1975. *Art and Nature.* Santa Barbara Museum of Natural History. Museum Talk. 49(1):2-13.

————. 1981. *The Art and Technique of Nature Printing.* Smithsonian Institution Touring Exhibit Service: Washington, D.C.

Hughes, S. 1978. *Washi. The World of Japanese Paper.* Kodansha: Tokyo.

————. 1981. *Fish Heads and Other Rubbings From Nature.* Santa Barbara Magazine. 7(4):72-79.

Kume, Y. 1980. *Tesuki Washi Shuho—Fine Handmade Papers of Japan.* Yoshodo Booksellers, Ltd.: Tokyo.

Little, R. W. 1976. *Nature Printing.* Pickwick-Morcroft: Pittsburgh.

Saium, Y., Ed. 1975. *Introduction to Gyotaku for Sport Fishermen.* Japan Publications: Tokyo. (In Japanese)

Simons, C. 1981. *Behold the Ones That Didn't Get Away.* Smithsonian. 12(3):151-153.

St. Maur, E. 1956. *The Fish Print.* Sports Illustrated. 4(25):52-54.